# RHYMES FOR
# MY RAGS

# BY ROBERT SERVICE

## VERSE

*Carols of an Old Codger*
*Songs for My Supper*
*Rhymes of a Rebel*
*Lyrics of a Lowbrow*
*The Spell of the Yukon*
*Ballads of a Cheechako*
*Rhymes of a Rolling Stone*
*Rhymes of a Red Cross Man*
*Ballads of a Bohemian*
*Bar-Room Ballads*
*Collected Verse*
*Songs of a Sun-Lover*
*Rhymes of a Roughneck*
*More Collected Verse*

––––––––––

## NOVELS

*The Trail of '98*
*The Pretender*
*The Poisoned Paradise*
*The Roughneck*
*The Master of the Microbe*
*The House of Fear*

## MISCELLANEOUS

*Why Not Grow Young?*

## AUTOBIOGRAPHY

*Ploughman of the Moon*
*Harper of Heaven*

# RHYMES FOR MY RAGS

BY ROBERT SERVICE

DODD, MEAD & COMPANY · NEW YORK

## PRELUDE

*Because the rhymes I make for raiment*
*Fail to avail its meed of payment,*
*I fain must make my well-worn tweeds*
*Suffice me for tomorrow's needs—*
*Until my verse the public reads.*

*I used to go to Savile Row,*
*But now their prices are so high,*
*With royalties at all time low,*
*Because my books few want to buy . . .*
*No, I don't blame them, but that's why.*

*Well, anyway I'd rather fare*
*In tattered rags and ring my chimes*
*Than strut around in wealthy wear.*
*—So in these tough and trying times*
*Let me flaunt like defiant flags*
*The jubilation of my RAGS.*

# CONTENTS

## LYRICS FOR LEVITY

## DERISIVE DITTIES

## RHYMES FOR RESIGNATION

## SONGS FOR SERENITY

# SONGS OF A GRAND-SIRE

# OLD CODGER

Of garden truck he made his fare,
    As his bright eyes bore witness;
Health was his habit and his care,
    His hobby human fitness.
He sang the praise of open sky,
    The gladth of Nature's giving;
And when at last he came to die
    It was of too long living.

He held aloof from hate and strife,
    Drank peace in dreamful doses;
He never voted in his life,
    Loved children, dogs and roses.
Let tyrants romp in gory glee,
    And revolutions roister,
He passed his days as peacefully
    As friar in a cloister.

So fellow sinners, should you choose
    Of doom to be a dodger,
At eighty be a bland recluse
    Like this serene old codger,
Who turned his back on fear and fret,
    And died nigh eighty-seven . . .
His name was—Robert Service: let
    Us hope he went to Heaven.

# MAMMY

I often wonder how
        Life clicks because
They don't make women now
        Like Mammy was.
When broods of two or three
        Content most men,
How wonderful was she
        With children ten!

Though sixty years have gone,
        As I look back,
I see her rise at dawn,
        Our boots to black;
Pull us from drowsy bed,
        Wet sponge to pass,
And speed us porridge fed
        To morning class.

Our duds to make and mend,
        Far into night,
O'er needle she would spend
        By bleary light.
Yet as her head drooped low,
        With withered hair,
It seemed the candle glow
        Made halo there.

And so with silvered pow
    I sigh because
They don't make women now
    Like Mammy was.

# LINDY LOU

If the good King only knew,
           Lindy Lou,
What a cherub child are you,
           It is true,
He would step down from his throne,
And would claim you for his own,
Then whatever would I do,
           Lindy Lou?

As I kiss your tiny feet,
           Lindy Lou,
I just feel I want to eat
           All of you.
What's so heaven-sweet and mild
As a happy baby-child?
If you died I would die too,
           Lindy Lou.

What's so lovely on this earth,
           Lindy Lou,
As your innocence and mirth
           Shining through?
Let us all do what we may
To make little children gay,
Heaven-happy, just as you,
           Lindy Lou.

# THE OLD GENERAL

Little Annabelle to please,
    (Lacking grace, I grant),
Grandpa down on hands and knees
    Plays the elephant.
Annabelle shrieks with delight,
    Bouncing up and down,
On his back and holding tight
    To his dressing gown.

As they roll and bowl along,
    Round and round the room,
There is sunshine and a song
    'Spite December gloom.
Yet we hear not Grandpa's groans,
    Hushed his beard inside,
As his old rheumatic bones
    Ache with every stride.

He has known his golden days,
    Soldiered with the best;
And to prove the people's praise
    Medals bright his breast.
Yet though his renown we chant,
    How we love him well
When he plays the elephant
    Just for Annabelle!

# MISS MISCHIEVOUS

Miss Don't-do-this and Don't-do-that
    Has such a sunny smile
You cannot help but chuckle at
    Her cuteness and her guile.
Her locks are silken floss of gold,
    Her eyes are pansy blue:
Maybe of years to eighty old
    The best is two.

Miss Don't-do-this and Don't-do-that
    To roguishness is fain;
To guard that laughter-loving brat
    Is quite a strain;
But when she tires of prank and play
    And says good-night,
I'm longing for another day
    Of child delight.

Miss Don't-do-this and Don't-do-that
    Will grow up soon.
I hope she'll never throw her hat
    Athwart the moon.
Yet I'll be sorrowful indeed,
    Remembering a day
Before she learned to humbly heed
    The word OBEY.

# BALLOON

I bought my little grandchild Ann
        A bright balloon,
And I was such a happy man
        To hear her croon.
She laughed and babbled with delight,
        So gold its glow,
As by a thread she held it tight,
        Then—let it go.

As if it gloried to be free
        It climbed the sky;
But oh how sorrowful was she,
        And sad was I!
And when at eve with sobbing cry
        She saw the moon,
She pleaded to the pensive sky
        For her balloon.

O Little One, I pray that you
        In years to be,
Will hold a tiny baby too,
        And know its glee;
That yours will always be the thrill
        And joy of June,
And that you never, never will
        Cry for the moon.

# SUSIE

My daughter Susie, aged two,
    Apes me in every way,
For as my household chores I do
    With brooms she loves to play.
A scrubbing brush to her is dear;
    Ah! Though my soul it vex,
My bunch of cuteness has, I fear,
        Kitchen complex.

My dream was that she might go far,
    And play or sing or dance;
Aye, even be a movie star
    Of glamour and romance.
But no more with such hope I think,
    For now her fondest wish is
To draw a chair up to the sink
        And wash the dishes.

Yet when you put it to a test
    In ups and downs of life,
A maiden's mission may be best
    To make a good house-wife;
To bake, to cook, to knit, to lave:
    And so I pray that Sue
Will keep a happy hearth and have
        A baby too.

# YOUNG MOTHER

Her baby was so full of glee,
   And through the day
It laughed and babbled on her knee
   In happy play.
It pulled her hair all out of curl
   With noisy joy;
So peppy she was glad her girl
   Was not a boy.

Then as she longed for it to sleep,
   To her surprise
It just relaxed within her keep
   With closing eyes.
And as it lay upon her breast
   So still its breath,
So exquisite its utter rest
   It looked like death.

It seemed like it had slipped away
   To shadow land;
With tiny face like tinted clay
   And waxen hand.
No ghost of sigh, no living look . . .
   Then with an ache
Of panic fear and love she shook
   Her babe awake.

# NATURE'S TOUCH

In kindergarten classed
        Dislike they knew;
And as the years went past
        It grew and grew;
Until in maidenhood
        Each sought a mate,
Then venom in their mood
        Was almost hate.

The lure of love they learned
        And they were wed;
Yet when they met each turned
        Away a head;
Each went her waspish way
        With muted damns—
Until they met one day
        With baby prams.

Then lo! Away was swept
        The scorn of years;
Hands clasped they almost wept
        With gentle tears.
Forgetting hateful days,
        All mother mild,
Each took with tender praise
        The other's child.

And now they talk of milk,
      Of diapers and such;
Of baby bosoms silk
      And tender to the touch.
A gemlike girl and boy,—
      With hope unsaid,
Each thinks with mother joy:
      'May these two wed!'

## STRIP TEASER

My precious grand-child, aged two,
Is eager to unlace one shoe,
      And then the other;
Her cotton socks she'll deftly doff,
Despite the mild reproaches of
      Her mother.

Around the house she loves to fare,
And with her rosy tootsies bare,
      Pit-pat the floor;
And though remonstrances we make
She presently decides to take
      Off something more.

Her pinafore she next unties,
And then before we realise,
      Her dress drops down;
Her panties and her *brassiere,*
Her chemise and her underwear
      Are round her strown.

And now she dances all about,
As naked as a new-caught trout,
      With impish glee;
And though she's beautiful like that,
(A cherubim, but not so fat),
      Quite shocked are we.

And so we dread with dim dismay
Some day she may her charms display
     In skimpy wear;
Aye, even in a gee-string she
May frolic on the stage of the
     *Folies-Bèrgere.*

But e'er she does, I hope she'll read
This worldly wise and warning screed,
     That to conceal,
Unto the ordinary man
Is often more alluring than
     To ALL reveal.

# RAGETTY DOLL

Rosemary has of dolls a dozen,
    Yet she disdains them all;
While Marie Rose, her pauper cousin
    Has just an old rag doll.
But you should see her mother it,
    And with her kisses smother it.

A twist of twill, a hank of hair,
    Fit for the rubbish bin;
How Rosemary with scorn would stare
    At its pathetic grin!
Yet Marie Rose can lover it,
    And with her kisses cover it.

Rosemary is a pampered pet;
    She sniffs a dainty nose
Of scorn at ragged dolls, and yet
    My love's with Marie Rose,
In garret corner shy and sweet,
    With rag doll Marguerite.

Though kin they are, a gulf will grow
    Between them with the years;
For one a life of love will know,
    The other toil and tears:
Perhaps that shabby rag doll knows
    The rue of Marie Rose.

# GIGNOL

Addict of Punch and Judy shows
        I was when I was small;
My kiddy laughter, I suppose,
        Rang louder than them all.
The Judge with banter I would bait,
        The Copper was a wretch;
But oh how I would hiss my hate
        For grim Jack Ketch.

Although a grandsire grey I still
        Love Punch and Judy shows,
And with my toddlers help to fill
        Enthusiastic rows.
How jolly is their mirth to see,
        And what a sigh they fetch,
When Punch begs to be shown and he
        Jerks up Jack Ketch.

Heigh ho! No more I watch the play;
        It is the audience
That gives me my delight today,—
        Such charm of innocence!
Immortal mimes! It seems to me,
        Could I re-live my span,
With gusto I would like to be
        A Punch and Judy Man.

# A SNIFTER

After working hard all day
    In the office,
How much worse on homeward way
    My old cough is!
Barney's Bar is gaily lit,
    Let me stop there;
Just to buck me up a bit
    Have a drop there.

As I stand beside the screen
    Hesitating,
I have thought of how Noreen
    Will be waiting;
Baby Patsy in her lap
    Gay and laughing,
While at Barney's foaming tap
    I am quaffing.

Barney's Bar is mighty bright,
    Looks so cheery.
Wonder what I'll drink tonight?
    Gee! I'm weary.
Will I have Scotch or Rye?
    Bourbon maybe . . .
Then I see with mental eye
    Wife and baby.

So I say 'tis malted milk
      I'll be skoffin';
Sooth my throttle sleek as silk,
      Ease my coughin' . . .
Say, I love them two to death,
      Sure they miss me:
With no whisky on my breath
      How they'll kiss me!

# SECOND CHILDHOOD

When I go on my morning walk,
    Because I'm mild,
If I be in the mood to talk
    I choose a child.
I'd rather prattle with a lass
    Of tender age
Than converse in the high-brow class
    With college sage.

I love the touch of silken hand
    That softly clings;
In old of age I understand
    Life's little things.
I love the lisp of tiny tongue
    And trusting eyes;
These are the joys that keep me young
    As daylight dies.

For as to second childhood I
    Draw gently near,
With happy heart I see the why
    Children are dear.
So wise Professor, go your way,—
    I am beguiled
To wistful loving by the gay
    Laugh of a child.

# TWO CHILDREN

Give me your hand, oh little one!
    Like children be we two;
Yet I am old, my day is done
    That barely breaks for you.
A baby-basket hard you hold,
    With in it cherries four:
You cherish them as men do gold,
      And count them o'er.

And then you stumble in your walk;
    The cherries scattered lie.
You pick them up with foolish talk
    And foolish glad am I,
When you wipe one quite clean of dust
    And give it unto me;
So in the baby-basket just
    Are three.

All this is simple, I confess,
    A moment piled with peace;
Yet loving men have died for less,
    And will till time shall cease. . . .
A silken hand in crinkled one—
    O Little Innocence!
O blessed moment in the sun
    E'er I go hence!

*RHYMES FOR REALITY*

# LOCAL LAD

I never saw a face so bright
    With brilliant blood and joy,
As was the grinning mug last night
    Of Dick, our local boy,
When with a clumsy, lucky clout
    He knocked the champion out.

A week ago he swung a pick
    And sweated in a ditch.
Tonight he's togged up mighty slick,
    And fancies himself rich.
With floozies, fine food, bubbly drink
    He'll go to hell I think.

Unless they make another match;
    And if they do I guess
The champion won't have a scratch,
    But Dick will be a mess;
His map will be a muck of gore
    As he sprawls on the floor.

Then he'll go back his pick to swing,
    And sweat deep in the mud . . .
Yet still I see him in the ring,
    So gay with glee and blood,
Dancing a jig and holding high
    His gloves to climb the sky.

# FINNIGAN'S FINISH

They thought I'd be a champion;
    They boasted loud of me.
A dozen victories I'd won,
    The Press was proud of me.
I saw myself with glory crowned,
    And would, beyond a doubt,
Till last night in the second round
    A Dago knocked me out.

It must have been an accident;
    I cannot understand.
For I was so damn confident
    I'd lick him with one hand.
I bounded in the ring to cheers;
    I panted for the fray:
Ten minutes more with hoots and jeers
    They bore me limp away.

I will not have the nerve to face
    The sporting mob today;
The doll I fell for—my disgrace
    Will feel and fade away.
Last night upon the brink of fame
    No favour did I lack:
Tomorrow from the sink of shame
    I'll beg my old job back.

# CARDIAC

A mattock high he swung;
I watched him at his toil;
With never gulp of lung
He gashed the ruddy soil.
Thought I, I'd give my wealth
       To have his health.

With fortune I would part,
And privilege resign,
Could I but have his heart,
And he have mine . . .
Then suddenly I knew
       My wish was true.

Like him I swung: with awe
He marked my steady breath.
Then suddenly I saw
That he was sick to death.
My heart in him was frail
       And seemed to fail.

Said I: 'Take back your heart
And I will bear with mine.
Poor lad! All wealth apart
'Tis murder I design.
Not all a Nabob's wealth
       Is worth your health.'

# SECRETARY

My Master is a man of might
    With manners like a hog;
He makes me slave from morn to night
    And treats me like a dog.
He thinks there's nothing on this earth
    His money cannot buy,
And claims to get full wages worth
    From hirelings such as I.

But does he? Though a Man of State,
    And fabulously rich,
He little guesses that his mate
    Is just a bonny bitch.
For he is grey and gross and fat,
    While I am tall and slim,
And when he's gone it happens that
    I take the place of him.

Oh God! The beauty of the blow
    When I will blast his life;
When I will laugh and let him know
    My mistress is his wife.
Today a doormat for his feet,
    He loves to see me squirm . . .
Tomorrow,—how revenge is sweet!
    The turning of the worm.

# FOUR-FOOT SHELF

'Come, see,' said he, 'my four-foot shelf,
      A forty volume row;
And every one I wrote myself,
      But that, of course, you know.'
I stared, I searched a memory dim,
      For though an author too,
Somehow I'd never heard of him,—
      None of his books I knew.

Said I: 'I'd like to borrow one,
      Fond memories to recall.'
Said he: 'I'll gladly give you *some,*
      And autograph them all.'
And so a dozen books he brought,
      And signed tome after tome:
Of course I thanked him quite a lot,
      And took them home.

So now I have to read his work,
      Though dry as dust it be;
No portion of it may I shirk,
      Lest he should question me.
This tale is true,—although it looks
      To me a bloody shame,
A guy could father forty books,
      Yet no one know his name.

# THE ACTOR

Enthusiastic was the crowd
    That hailed him with delight;
The wine was bright, the laughter loud
    And glorious the night.
But when at dawn he drove away
    With echo of their cheer,
To where his little daughter lay,
    Then he knew— Fear.

How strangely still the house! He crept
    On tip-toe to the bed;
And there she lay as if she slept
    With candles at her head.
Her mother died to give her birth,
    An angel child was she;
To him the dearest one on earth . . .
    How could it be?

'O God! If she could only live,'
    He thought with bitter pain,
'How gladly, gladly would I give
    My glory and my gain.
I have created many a part,
    And many a triumph known;
Yet here is one with breaking heart
    I play alone.'

Beside the hush of her his breath
    Came with a sobbing sigh.
He babbled: 'Sweet, you play at death . . .
    'Tis I who die.'

# THE HOMICIDE

They say she speeded wanton wild
    When she was warm with wine;
And so she killed a little child,
    (Could have been yours or mine).
The Judge's verdict was not mild,
    And heavy was the fine.

And yet I see her driving still,
    But maybe with more care . . .
Oh I should hate a child to kill
    With vine leaves in my hair:
I think that I should grieve until
    Life was too bleak to bear.

I think that I would see each day
    That child in beauty grow.
How she would haunt me in her play.
    And I would watch her go
To school a-dancing on her way,
    With gladness all aglow!

And then one day I might believe,
    With angel eyes ashine,
She'd say to me: 'Please do not grieve,
    Maybe the fault was mine.
Take heart,—to Heaven's comfort cleave,
    For am I not divine!'

I think I know how I would feel
        If I a child should slay;
The rest of living I would kneel
        And for God's pity pray . . .
*Madam, I saw you at the wheel*
        *Of your new car today.*

# THE JUDGEMENT

The Judge looked down, his face was grim,
  He scratched his ear;
The gangster's moll looked up at him
  With eyes of fear.
She thought: 'This guy in velvet gown,
  With balding pate,
Who now on me is looking down,
  Can seal my fate.'

The Judge thought: 'Fifteen years or ten
  I might decree.
Just let me say the word and then
  Go home to tea.
But then this poor wretch might not be
  So long alive . . .'
So with surprise he heard that he
  Was saying 'Five.'

The Judge went home.  His daughter's child
  Was five that day;
And with sweet gifts around her piled
  She laughed in play.
Then mused the Judge: 'Life oft bestows
  Such evil odds.
May he who human mercy shows
  Not count on God's?'

# POOR POET

'A man should write to please himself,'
        He proudly said.
Well, see his poems on the shelf,
        Dusty, unread.

When he came to my shop each day,
        So peaked and cold,
I'd sneak one of his books away
        And say 'twas sold.

And then by chance he looked below,
        And saw a stack
Of his own work,—speechless with woe
        He came not back.

I hate to think he took to drink,
        And passed away;
I have not heard of him a word
        Unto this day.

A man must write to please himself,
        Of all it's true;
But happy they who spurning pelf—
        Please people too.

# TIM

My brother Tim has children ten,
    While I have none.
Maybe that's why he's toiling when
    To ease I've won.
But though I would some of his brood
    Give hearth and care,
I know that not a one he would
    Have heart to spare.

'Tis children that have kept him poor;
    He's clad them neat.
They've never wanted, I am sure,
    For bite to eat.
And though their future may be dim,
    They laugh a lot.
Am I tearful for Brother Tim?
    Oh no, I'm not.

I know he goes to work each day
    With flagging feet.
'Tis hard, even with decent pay,
    To make ends meet.
But when my sterile home I see,
    So smugly prim,
Although my banker bows to me,
    I envy Tim.

# BRAVE COWARD

Elisabeth imagines I've
    A yellow streak.
She deems I have no dash and drive,
    Jest dogoned weak.
'A man should be a man,' says Liz
    'Trade blow for blow.'
Poor kid! What my position is,
    She jest don't know.

She jest don't know my old man killed,
    Yea, slew and slew.
As steamy blood he sweetly spilled,
    So could I too.
And though no wrath of heart I show
    When I see red,
I fear no S. O. B. but oh
    Myself I dread.

Though fellers reckon me a dope
    And trigger-shy,
'Tain't nice to dangle on a rope,
    And like Pa die.
So as I belly to the bar
    Meek is my breath . . .
No guts! —Don't needle me too far,
    Elizabeth!

# FIDELITY

Being a shorty, as you see,
     A bare five footer,
The why my wife is true to me
     Is my six-shooter.
For every time a guy goes by
     Who looks like a lover,
I polish it to catch his eye,
     And spin it over.

He notes its notches as I say:
     'Believe me, Brother,
If Junie ever goes astray,
     They'll be another.'
A husband has to have a gun
     And guts to pull it:
Few fellows think a bit of fun
     Is worth a bullet.

For June would sit on any knee
     If it wore pants,
Yet she is faithful unto me,
     As gossip grants.
And though I know some six-foot guy
     Would better suit her,
Her virtue triumphs, thanks to my
     Six-shooter.

# A BACHELOR

'Why keep a cow when I can buy,'
        Said he, 'the milk I need,'
I wanted to spit in his eye
        Of selfishness and greed;
But did not, for the reason he
        Was stronger than I be.

I told him: ' 'Tis our human fate,
        For better or for worse,
That man and maid should love and mate,
        And little children nurse.
Of course, if you are less than man
        You can't do what we can.

'So many loving maids would wed,
        And wondrous mothers be.'
'I'll buy the love I want,' he said,
        'No squally brats for me.'
. . . I hope the devil stoketh well
        For him a special hell.

# LOTTERY TICKET

'A ticket for the lottery
I've purchased every week,' said she
  'For years a score
Though desperately poor am I,
Oh how I've scrimped and scraped to buy
  One chance more.

'Each week I think I'll gain the prize,
And end my sorrows and my sighs,
  For I'll be rich;
Then nevermore I'll eat bread dry,
With icy hands to cry and cry
  And stitch and stitch.'

'Tis true she won the premier prize;
It was of formidable size,
  Ten million francs.
I know, because the man who sold
It to her splenically told
  He got no thanks.

The lucky one was never found,
For she was snugly underground,
  And minus breath;
And with that ticket tucked away,
In some old stocking, so they say,
  She starved to death.

# SAILOR'S SWEETHEART

He sleeps beside me in the bed;
Upon my breast I hold his head;
Oh how I would that we were wed,
   For he sails in the morning.

I wish I had not been so kind;
But love is fain and passion blind,
While out of sight is out of mind,
   And he ships in the morning.

I feel his bairn stir in my womb;
Poor wee one, born to bitter doom;
How dreary dark will be the gloom,
   When he goes in the morning!

A sailor lad has need to court
A loving lass in every port;
To him it's just a bit of sport . . .
   My heart-break's in the morning.

# FAILURE

He wrote a play; by day and night
He strove with passion and delight;
Yet knew, long ere the curtain drop,
His drama was a sorry flop.

In Parliament he sought a seat;
Election Day brought dire defeat;
Yet he had wooed with word and pen
Prodigiously his fellow men.

And then he wrote a lighter play
That made him famous in a day.
He won a seat in Parliament,
And starry was the way he went.

Yet as he neared the door of death
They heard him say with broken breath:
'For all I've spoken, planned and penned,
I'm just a wash-out in the end.'

So are we all; our triumphs won
Are mean by what we might have done.
Our victories that men applaud
Are sordid in the sight of God.

# MY SON

I must not let my boy Dick down,
      Knight of the air.
With wings of light he won renown
      Then crashed somewhere.
To fly to France from London town
      I do not dare.

Oh he was such a simple lad
      Who loved the sky;
A modern day Sir Galahad,
      No need to die:
Earthbound he might have been so glad,
      Yet chose to fly.

I ask from where his courage stemmed?
      I've never flown;
Air-travel I have oft condemned,—
      Now I'm alone,
Yet somehow hold the bright belief
      God gave his brief.

So now I must live up to him
      Who won on high
A lustre time will never dim;
      Though coward I,
Let me revere till life be done
      My hero son.

# AUNT JANE

When Aunt Jane died we hunted round,
And money everywhere we found.
How much I do not care to say,
But no death duties will we pay,
And Aunt Jane will be well content
We bilked the bloody Government.

While others spent she loved to save,
But couldn't take it to her grave.
While others save we love to spend;
She hated us but in the end
Because she left no Testament
To us all her possessions went.

That is to say they did not find
A lawyer's Will of any kind.
Yet there was one in her own hand,
A Home for Ailing Cats she planned.
Well, you can understand my ire:
Promptly I put it in the fire.

In misery she chose to die,
Yet we will make her money fly.
And as we mourn for poor Aunt Jane
The thought alleviates our pain:
Perhaps her savings in the end
Gave her more joy than we who spend.

# THE ARTIST

All day with brow of anxious thought
    The dictionary through,
Amid a million words he sought
    The sole one that would do.
He wandered on from pub to pub
    Yet never ceased to seek
With burning brain and pencil stub
    The Word Unique.

Said he: 'I'll nail it down or die.
    Oh Heaven help me, pray!'
And then a heavy car dashed by,
    And he was in the way.
They rushed him to the hospital,
    And though his chance was bleak,
He cried: 'I'll croak, but find I shall
    The Word Unique.'

They reckoned he was off his head,
    And could be it was so;
For as they bent above his bed
    He mumbled soft and low.
And then a name they heard him speak,
    Yet did not deem it odd . . .
At last he'd found the Word Unique,—
    Just God.

# BELATED CONSCIENCE

To buy for school a copy-book
    I asked my Dad for two-pence;
He gave it with a gentle look,
    Although he had but few pence.
'Twas then I proved myself a crook
    And came a moral cropper,
I bought a penny copy-book
    And blued the other copper.

I spent it on a sausage roll
    Gulped down with guilt suggestion,
To the damnation of my soul
    And awful indigestion.
Poor Dad! His job was hard to hold;
    His mouths to feed were many;
Were he alive a millionfold
    I'd pay him for his penny.

Now nigh the grave I think with grief,
    Though other sins are many,
I am a liar and a thief
    'Cause once I stole a penny:
Yet be he pious as a friar
    It is my firm believing,
That every man has been a liar
    And most of us done thieving.

# OLD ENGINE DRIVER

For five and twenty years I've run
      A famous train;
But now my spell of speed is done,
      No more I'll strain
My sight along the treadless tracks,
      The gleamy rails:
My hand upon the throttle slacks,
      My vision fails.

No more I'll urge my steed of steel
      Through hostile night;
No more the mastery I'll feel
      Of monster might.
I'll miss the hiss of giant steam,
      The clank, the roar;
The agony of brakes that scream
      I'll hear no more.

Oh I have held within my hand
      A million lives;
And now my son takes command
      And proudly drives;
While from my cottage wistfully
      I watch his train,
And wave and wave and seem to see
      Myself again.

# TO A TYCOON

Since much has been your mirth
   And fair your fate,
Friend, leave your lot of earth
   Less desolate.
With frailing overdue,
   Why don't you try
The bit of God in you
   To justify?

Try to discern the grace
   All greed above,
That may uplift the race
   To realm of love.
For in you is a spark,
   A heaven-glow,
That will illume the dark
   Before you go.

Aye, though it be that you
   To Faith are blind,
There's one thing you can do,
   It's—just be kind.
The anguish understand,
   Of hearts that bleed:
Friend, lend a helping hand
   To those in need.

# COMRADES

Three Holies sat in sacred place
        And quaffed celestial wine,
As they discussed the human race
        With dignity divine.
Said they: 'Although in doctrine we
        May differ more or less,
In spirit stoutly we agree
        Religion's a success.'

Said One: 'I praise the pride of war,
        The Faith that mocks at fear;
Desire of death in battle for
        It bringeth Heaven near.'
The Second said: ' 'Tis Peace I preach,
        And hate of human strife;
The sufferance of pain I teach,
        The sanctity of life.'

Then said the Third: 'Love I proclaim
        The goal of human good . . .
Yet are we not all three the same
        In holy brotherhood?'
And so they went forth hand in hand,
        Wending a starry way,—
Mohamet, gentle Buddha and
        He of Gethsemenè.

# SACRIFICE

I gave an eye to save from night
     A babe born blind;
And now with eager semi-sight
     Vast joy I find
To think a child can share with me
     Earth ecstasy!

Delight of dawn with dewy gleam
     On damask rose;
Crimson and gold as pennons stream
     Where sunset flows;
And sight most nigh to paradise,
     Star-studded skies.

Ah! How in old of age I feel,
     E'er end my days,
Could I star-splendoured sky reveal
     To childish gaze,
Not one eye would I give, but two,—
     *Well, wouldn't you?*

# LYRICS FOR LEVITY

# FAREWELL TO VERSE

In youth when oft my muse was dumb,
    My fancy nighly dead,
To make my inspiration come
    I stood upon my head;
And thus I let the blood down flow
    Into my cerebellum,
And published every Spring or so
    Slim tomes in vellum.

Alas! I am rheumatic now,
    Grey is my crown;
I can no more with brooding brow
    Stand upside-down.
I fear I might in such a pose
    Burst brain blood-vessel;
And that would be a woeful close
    To my rhyme wrestle.

If to write verse I must reverse
    I fear I'm stymied;
In ink of prose I must immerse
    A pen de-rhymèd.
No more to spank the lyric lyre
    Like Keats or Browning,
May I inspire the Sacred Fire
    By Upside-downing.

# TRIUMPH

Why am I full of joy although
    It drizzles on the links?
Why am I buying *Veuve Cliquot*,
    And setting up the drinks?
Why stand I like a prince amid
    My pals and envy none?
Ye gods of golf! Today I did
    A Hole in One.

I drove my ball to heaven high,
    It over-topped the hill;
I tried to guess how it would lie,
    If on the fairway still.
I climbed the rise, so sure I'd hit
    It straight towards the green:
I looked and looked,—no trace of it
    Was to be seen.

My partner putted to the pin,
    Then hoarse I heard him call;
And lo! So snug the hole within
    Gleamed up my ball.
Yea, it was mine. Oh what a thrill!
    What dandy drive I'd done
By luck,—well, grant a little skill,
    I'd holed in one.

Say that my score is eighty odd,
  And though I won't give up,—
Say that as round the course I plod,
  I never win a cup.
Say that my handicap's nineteen,
  And of my game make fun,
But holler: 'On the seventh green
  HE HOLED IN ONE.'

# PIPE SMOKER

Because I love the soothing weed
  And am of sober type,
I'd choose me for a friend in need
  A man who smokes a pipe.
A cove who hasn't much to say,
  And spits into the fire,
Puffing like me a pipe of clay,
  Corn-cob or briar.

A chap original of thought,
  With cheery point of view,
Who has of gumption quite a lot,
  And streaks of humour too.
He need not be a whiskered sage,
  With wisdom over-ripe:
Just give me in the old of age
  A pal who smokes a pipe.

A cigarette may make for wit,
  Although I like it not;
A good cigar, I must admit,
  Gives dignity to thought.
But as my glass of grog I sip
  I never, never gripe
If I have for companionship
  A guy who smokes a pipe.

# RELAX

Do you recall that happy hike
   With bundles on our backs?
How near to heaven it was like
   To blissfully relax!
In cosy tavern of good cheer
   To doff our heavy packs,
And with a mug of foamy beer
         Relax.

Learn to relax: to clean the mind
   Of fear and doubt and care,
And in vacuity to find
   The perfect peace that's there.
With lassitude of heart and hand,
   When every sinew slacks,
How good to rest the old bean and
         Relax, relax.

Just sink back in an easy chair
   For forty winks or so,
And fold your hands as if in prayer,
   —That helps a lot, you know.
Forget that you are you awhile,
   And pliable as wax,
Just beatifically smile . . .
      Relax, relax, relax.

# SUCCESSFUL FAILURE

I wonder if successful men
        Are always happy?
And do they sing with gusto when
        Springtime is sappy?
Although I am of snow-white hair
        And nighly mortal,
Each time I sniff the April air
        I chortle.

I wonder if a millionaire
        Jigs with enjoyment,
Having such heaps of time to spare
        For daft employment.
For as I dance the Highland Fling
        My glee is muckle,
And doping out new songs to sing
        I chuckle.

I wonder why so soon forgot
        Are fame and riches;
Let cottage comfort be my lot
        With well-worn britches.
As in a pub a poor unknown,
        Brown ale quaffing,
To think of all I'll never own,—
        I'm laughing.

# THE RECEPTIONIST

France is the fairest land on earth,
   Lovely to heart's desire,
And twice a year I span its girth,
   Its beauty to admire.
But when a pub I seek each night,
   To my profound vexation
On form they hand me I've to write
   My occupation.

So once in a derisive mood
   My pen I nibbled;
And though I know I never should:
   'Gangster' I scribbled.
But as the clerk with startled face
   Looked stark suspicion,
I blurred it out and in its place
   Put 'Politician.'

Then suddenly dissolved his frown;
   His face fused to a grin,
As humorously he set down
   The form I handed in.
His shrug was eloquent to view.
   Quoth he: 'What's in a name?
In France, alas! the lousy two
   Are just the same.'

# PROFANE POET

Oh how it would enable me
  To titillate my vanity
If you should choose to label me
  A Poet of Profanity!
For I've been known with vulgar slang
  To stoke the Sacred Fire,
And even used a word like 'hang',
   Suggesting ire.

Yea, I've been slyly told, although
  It savours of inanity,
In print the ladies often show
  A failing for profanity.
So to delight the dears I try,
  And often in the past
In fabricating sonnets I
   Have fulminated: 'Blast!'

I know I shock the sober folk
  Who doubt my lyric sanity,
And readers of my rhyme provoke
  By publishing profanity,
But oh a hale and hearty curse
  Is very dear to me,
And so I end this bit of verse
   With d— and d— and d—!

# FAMILIARITY

Familiarity some claim
      Can breed contempt,
So from it let it be your aim
      To be exempt.
Let no one exercise his brawn
      To slap your back,
Lest he forget your name is John,
      And call you Jack.

To those who crash your private pew
      Be sour as krout;
Don't let them see the real 'you,'
      And bawl you out.
Don't call your Cousin William—Bill,
      But formal be.
Have care! Beware and shun famil—
      Iarity.

I'm quite polite. My hat I doff
      But little say.
I give the crowd the big brush-off,
      And go my way.
To common folk I do not freeze,
      I am no snob:
But though my name is Robert, please
      Don't call me BOB.

## OBESITY

With belly like a poisoned pup
　　　Said I: 'I must give bacon up;
And also, I profanely fear,
　　　I must abandon bread and beer
That make for portliness they say;
　　　Yet of them copiously today
I ate with an increasingly sense
　　　　　Of grievous corpulence.

I like a lot of things I like.
　　　Too bad that I must go on strike
Against pork sausages and mash,
　　　Spaghetti and fried corn-beef hash.
I deem he is a lucky soul
　　　Who has no need of girth control;
For in the old of age: *'Il faut*
　　　　　*Souffrir pour etre beau.'*

Yet let me not be unconsoled:
　　　So many greybeards I behold,
Distinguished in affairs of State,
　　　In culture counted with the Great,
Have tummies with a shameless bulge,
　　　And so I think I'll still indulge
In eats I like without a qualm,
　　　　　And damn my diaphragm!

# TRIPE

When I was young and moron
        I doted on Hall Caine;
Corelli I would pore on,
        Despite high-brow disdain.
Aye, though them critic fellers
        Damned both in bitter type,
Insisting them best-sellers
        Were just Tripe.

Today I'm reading Cronin,
        Du Maurier and such,
And critics still are groanin'
        And griping overmuch.
But I, their scorn unheeding,
        Forget to light my pipe,
So rapt am I a-reading
        Of their Tripe.

For though my head is hoary,
        Still moron is my heart;
I love a darned good story
        With action from the start.
Aye, though the critics suffer
        And artistically gripe,
Just write me down a duffer
        Loving Tripe.

# TOURIST

'Twas in a village in Lorraine
    Whose name I quite forget,
I found I needfully was fain
    To buy a *serviette*.
I sought a shop wherein they sell
    Such articles as these,
And told a smiling mademoiselle;
    'I want a towel, please.'

'Of kinds,' said she, 'I've only two,'
    And took the bundles down;
And one was coloured azure blue,
    And one was khaki brown.
With doubt I scratched my hoary head;
    The quality was right;
The size too, yet I gravely said:
    'Too bad you haven't white.'

That pretty maid had sunny hair,
    Her gaze was free from guile,
And while I hesitated there
    She watched me with a smile.
Then as I went to take the blue
    She said 'Non' meaning no.
'Ze khaki ones are best, M'sieu:
    Ze *dirts* zey do not show.'

# THE BUYERS

Father drank himself to death,—
      Quite enjoyed it.
Urged to draw a sober breath
      He'd avoid it.
'Save your sympathy,' said Dad;
      'Never sought it.
Hob-nail liver, gay and glad,
      Sure,—I bought it.'

Uncle made a heap of dough,
      Ponies playing.
'Easy come and easy go,'
      Was his saying.
Though he died in poverty
      Fit he thought it,
Grinning with philosophy:
      'Guess I bought it.'

Auntie took the way of sin,
      Seeking pleasure;
Lovers came, her heart to win,
      Bearing treasure.
Sickness smote,—with lips that bled
      Brave she fought it;
Smiling on her dying bed:
      'Dears, I bought it.'

My decades of life are run,
    Eight precisely;
Yet I've lost a lot of fun
    Living wisely.
Too much piety don't pay,
    Time has taught it;
Hadn't guts to go astray;
Life's a bloody bore today,—
    Well, I've bought it.

# PROCREATION

It hurts my pride that I should be
    The issue of a night of lust;
Yet even Bishops, you'll agree,
    Obey the biologic 'must';
Though no doubt with more dignity
    Than we of layman dust.

I think the Lord made a mistake
    When he designed the human race,
That man and angel in the make
    Should have brutality for base.
Jehovah might have planned at least
    Not to confound us with the beast.

So with humiliation I
    Think of my basic origin;
And yet with some relief I sigh,—
    I might have been conceived in sin;
Instead of being, I believe,
    The offspring of a nuptial eve.

So when I look in beauty's face,
    Or that of king or saint or sage,
It seems to me I darkly trace
    Their being to a rutting rage . . .
Had I been Deity's adviser
    Meseems I might have planned it wiser.

# SPATS

When young I was a Socialist
        Despite my tender years;
No blessed chance I ever missed
        To slam the profiteers.
Yet though a fanatic I was,
        And cursed aristocrats,
The Party chucked me out because
        I sported Spats.

Aye, though on soap boxes I stood,
        And spouted in the parks,
They grizzled that my foot-wear would
        Be disavowed by Marx.
It's buttons of a pearly sheen
        *Bourgois* they deemed and thus
They told me; 'You must choose between
        Your spats and us.'

Alas! I loved my gaitered feet
        Of smoothly fitting fawn;
They were so snappy and so neat,
        A gift from Uncle John
Who had a fortune in the Bank
        That one day might be mine:
'Give up my spats!' said I, 'I thank
        You—but resign.'

Today when red or pink I see
       In stripy pants of state,
I think of how they lost in me
       A demon of debate.
I muse as Leaders strut about
       In frock-coats and high hats . . .
The bloody party chucked me out
       Because of Spats.

# THE SHORTER CATECHISM

I burned my fingers on the stove
        And wept with bitterness;
But poor old Auntie Maggie strove
        To comfort my distress.
Said she: 'Think, lassie, how you'll **burn**
        Like any wicked besom
In fires of hell if you don't learn
        Your Shorter Catechism.'

*A man's chief end is* it began,
        (No mention of a woman's),
*To glorify*—I think it ran,
        *The God who made poor humans.*
And as I learned, I thought: if this—
        (My distaste growing stronger),
The Shorter Catechism is,
        Lord save us from the longer.

The years have passed and I begin
        (Although I'm far from clever),
To doubt if when we die in sin
        Our bodies grill forever.
Now I've more surface space to burn,
        Since I am tall and lissom,
I think it's hell enough to learn
        The Shorter Catechism.

# THE BATTLE

*Dames should be doomed to dungeons*
*Who masticate raw onions.*

She was the cuddly kind of Miss
   A man can love to death;
But when I sought to steal a kiss
   I wilted from a breath
With onion odour so intense
   I lost my loving sense.

Yet she was ever in my thought
   Like some exotic flower,
And so a garlic bulb I bought
   And chewed it by the hour;
Then when we met I thrilled to see
   'Twas she who shrank from me.

So breath to breath we battled there,
   To dominate each other;
And though her onions odious were,
   My garlic was a smother;
Till loth I said: 'If we would kiss
   Let's call an armistice.

'Now we have proved that we are true
      To our opinions,
My garlic I'll give up if you
      Give up your onions.'
And so next day with honey sips
      How sweet her lips!

# ERICO

Oh darling Eric, why did you
For my fond affection sue,
And then with surgeons artful aid
Transform yourself into a maid?
So now in petticoats you go
And people call you Erico.

Sometimes I wonder if they can
Change me in turn into a man;
Then after all we might get wed
And frolic on a feather bed:
Although I do not see how we
Could ever have a family.

Oh dear! Oh dear! It's so complex.
Why must they meddle with our sex.
My Eric was a handsome 'he,'
But now he—oh excuse me—she
Informs me that I must forget
I was his blond Elizabet.

Alas! These scientists of Sweden
I curse, who've robbed me of my Eden;
Who with their weird hormones inhuman
Can make a man into a woman.
Alas, poor Eric! . . . Erico
I wish you were in Jerico.

# THE CENTENARIANS

*I asked of ancient gaffers three*
　　*The way of their ripe living,*
*And this is what they told to me*
　　*Without misgiving.*

*The First:* 'The why I've lived so long,
　　To my fond recollection
Is that for women, wine and song
　　I've had a predilection.
Full many a bawdy stave I've sung
　　With wenches of my choosing,
But of the joys that kept me young
　　The best was boozing.'

*The Second:* 'I'm a sage revered
　　Because I was a fool,
And with the bourgeon of my beard
　　I kept my ardour cool.
On health I have conserved my hold
　　By never dissipating:
And that is why a hundred old
　　I'm celebrating.'

*The Third:* 'The explanation I
          Have been so long a-olding,
Is that to wash I never try,
          Despite conjugal scolding.
I hate the sight of soap and so
          I seldom change my shirt:
Believe me, Brother, there is no
          Preservative like dirt.'

So there you have the reasons three
          Why age may you rejoice:
Booze, squalour and temerity,—
          Well, you may take your choice.
Yet let me say, although it may
          Your egoism hurt,
Of all the three it seems to me
          The best is DIRT.

# SURTAX

When I was young and Scottish I
   Allergic was to spending;
I put a heap of bawbees by,
   But now my life is ending,
Although I would my hoarded pelf
   Impetuously scatter,
Each day I live I find myself
   Financially fatter.

Though all the market I might buy,
   There's nothing to my needing;
I only have one bed to lie,
   One mouth for feeding.
So what's the good of all that dough
   Accumulating daily?
I should have spent it long ago
   In living gaily.

So take my tip, my prudent friend,
   Without misgiving;
Don't guard your fortune to the end,
   But blow it living.
Better on bubbly be it spent,
   And chorus cuties,
Than pay it to the Government
   For damned Death Duties.

# PLEBEIAN PLUTOCRAT

I own a gorgeous Cadillac,
  A chauffeur garbed in blue;
And as I sit behind his back
  His beefy neck I view.
Yet let me whisper, though you may
  Think me a queer old cuss,
From Claude I often sneak away
  To board a bus.

A democrat, I love the crowd,
  The bustle and the din;
The market wives who gab aloud
  As they go out and in.
I chuckle as I pay my dime,
  With mien meticulous:
You can't believe how happy I'm;
  Aboard a bus.

The driver of my Cadillac
  Has such a haughty sneer;
I'm sure he would give me the sack
  If he beheld me here.
His horror all my friends would share
  Could they but see me thus:
A gleeful multi-millionaire
  Aboard a bus.

# JANE

My daughter Jane makes dresses
For beautiful Princesses;
But though she's plain is Jane,
Of needlework she's vain,
And makes such pretty things
For relatives of Kings.

She reads the picture papers
Where Royalties cut capers,
And often says to me:
'How wealthy they must be,
That nearly every day
A new robe they can pay.'

Says I: 'If your Princesses
Could *fabric* pretty dresses,
Though from a throne they stem
I would think more of them.
Peeress and shopgirl are
To my mind on a par.'

Says Jane: 'But for their backing
I might be sewing sacking.
Instead, I work with joy
In exquisite employ,
Embroidering rich dresses
For elegant Princesses . . .
Damn social upsetters
Who criticise their betters!'

# WASHERWIFE

The aged Queen who passed away
Had sixty servants, so they say;
Twice sixty hands her shoes to tie:
Two soapy ones have I.

The old Queen had of beds a score;
A cot have I and ask no more.
For when the last is said and done
One can but die in one.

The old Queen rightly thought that she
Was better than the likes o' me;
And yet I'm glad despite her grace
I am not in her place.

The old Queen's gone and I am here,
To eat my tripe and drink my beer,
Athinkin' as I wash my clothes:
We must have monarchs, I suppose . . .
Well, well,—'Taint no skin off my nose!

# LAND MINE

A grey gull hovered overhead,
    Then wisely flew away.
'In half a jiffy you'll be dead,'
    I thought I heard it say;
As there upon the railway line,
    Checking an urge to cough,
I laboured to de-fuse the mine
    That had not yet gone off.

I tapped around the time-clock rim,
    Then something worried me.
I heard the singing of a hymn:
    *Nearer my God to Thee.*
That damned Salvation Army band!
    I phoned back to the boys:
'Please tell them,—they will understand,—
    Cut out the bloody noise!'

Silence . . . I went to work anew,
    And then I heard a tick
That told me the blast was due,—
    I never ran so quick.
I heard the fury-roar behind;
    The earth erupted hell,
As hoisted high and stunned and blind
    Into a ditch I fell.

Then when at last I crawled from cover,
    My hands were bloody raw;
And I was blue and bruised all over,
    And this is what I saw:
All pale, but panting with elation,
    And very much unstuck,
There was the Army of Salvation
    Emerging from the muck.

And then I heard the Captain saying:
    ' 'Twas Heaven heard our pleas;
For there anight we all were praying
    Down on our bended knees.
'Twas little hope your comrades gave you,
    Though we had faith divine . . .
The blessed Lord stooped down to save you,
    But Gosh! *He cut it fine.*'

# THE BIOLOGIC URGE

Confound all aberrations which
      Make men do foolish things,
Like buying bracelets for a bitch,
      Or witless wedding rings.
As if we had not woe enough
      Our simple souls to vex,
Without that brand of trouble stuff
      We label Sex.

Has science not the means produced
      For human propagation,
By artificially induced
      Insemination?
Then every man might be a priest,
      And every maid a nun . . .
Oh well, as chaste as they at least,—
      But nix on fun.

Just think how we would grow in grace
      If lust we could exclude;
Then innocence might take its place,
      —Well, in a sense it could.
How we would be forever free
      From passions that perplex!
What peace on earth if only we
      Could outlaw Sex!

# TREAT 'EM ROUGH

First time I dared propose,
        A callow lad was I;
I donned my Sunday clothes,
        I wore my Old School Tie.
Awaiting me Louise
        Was dolled to beat the band,
So going on my knees
        I begged her hand.

Oh yes, she gave me her hand,—
        A box upon the ear;
I could not understand,
        I blinked away a tear.
Then scornfully she said:
        'Next time you kneel before
A maid, young man don't spread
        Your hankey on the floor.'

So next time I proposed,
        Thinks I, I'll treat 'em rough.
Her name was Lily Rose,
        I gave her he-man stuff.
I yanked her on my knee,
        And as her ear I bit,
To my amazement she
        Seemed to like it.

The old cave-men knew best;
     Grab girlies by the hair,
And though they may protest
     Drag them into your lair.
So young men seeking mates,
     Take my tip, if rejected:
A modern maid just hates
     To be respected.

## COWS

I love to watch my seven cows
In meads of buttercups abrowse,
        With guilded knees;
But even more I love to see
Them chew the cud so tranquilly
        In twilight ease.

Each is the image of content
From fragrant hours in clover spent,
        'Mid leaf and bud;
As up and down without a pause
Mechanically move their jaws
        To chew the cud.

Friend, there's a hope for me and you:
Let us resolve to chew and chew
        With molars strong;
The man who learns to masticate
With patience may control his fate,
        His life prolong.

In salivation is salvation:
So if some silly little nation
      Should bathe in blood,
Let's take a lesson from the cow,
And learn in life's long gloaming how
      To chew the cud.

# DARK GLASSES

Sweet maiden, why disguise
The beauty of your eyes
        With glasses black?
Although I'm well aware
That you are more than fair,
        Allure you lack.
For as I stare at you
I ask if brown or blue
        Your optics are?
But though I cannot see,
I'm sure that each must be
        Bright as a star.

They may be green or grey,
'Tis very hard to say,
        Or violet;
The lovelight in their glow
Alas, I'll never know,
        To my regret.
In some rhyme-book I've read,
A lady bard has said,
        And deemed it true,
Men will not bite the necks
Of sweeties who wear specs,—
        Young man, would you?

But though they balk romance,
Columbus took a chance,
      And so would I;
Even with orbs unseen
I'd fain make you my queen
      And you en-sky.
Alas I see you go,
And I will never know
      Your pupils tint;
So o'er a lonely drink
I force myself to think:
      Damsel, you squint!

# POET AND PEER

They asked the Bard of Ayr to dine;
The banquet hall was fit and fine,
　　　With gracing it a Lord;
The poet came; his face was grim
To find the place reserved for him
　　　Was at the butler's board.

So when the gentry called him in,
He entered with a knavish grin
　　　And sipped a glass of wine;
But when they asked would he recite
Something of late he'd chanced to write
　　　He ettled to decline.

Then with a sly, sardonic look
He opened up a little book
　　　Containing many a gem;
And as they sat in raiment fine,
So smug and soused with rosy wine,
　　　This verse he read to them.

*'You see yon birkie caw'ed a Lord,*
　　　*Who struts and stares an' a' that,*
*Though hundreds worship at his word*
　　　*He's but a coof for a' that.*
*For a' that and a' that,*
　　　*A man's a man for a' that.*

He pointed at that portly Grace
Who glared with apoplectic face,
     While others stared with gloom;
Then having paid them all he owed,
Burns, Bard of Homespun, smiled and strode
     Superbly from the room.

## TOILET SEATS

While I am emulating Keats
My brother fabrics toilet seats,
The which, they say, are works of art,
Aesthetic features of the mart;
So exquisitely are they made
With plastic of a pastel shade,
Of topaz, ivory or rose,
Inviting to serene repose.

Rajahs I'm told have seats of gold,—
(They must, I fear, be very cold).
But Tom's have thermostatic heat,
With sympathy your grace to greet.
Like silver they are neon lit,
Making a halo as you sit:
Then lo! they play with dulset tone
A melody by Mendelssohn.

Oh were I lyrical as Yeats
I would not sing of toilet seats,
But rather serenade a star,—
Yet I must take things as they are.
For even kings must coyly own
Them as essential as a throne:
So as I tug the Muse's teats
I envy Tom his toilet seats.

# DISTRACTED DRUGGIST

'A shilling's worth of quinine, please,'
      The customer demanded.
The druggist went down on his knees
      And from a cupboard handed
The waiting man a tiny flask:
      'Here, Sir, is what you ask.'


The buyer paid and went away,
      The druggist rubbed his glasses,
Then sudden shouted in dismay:
      'Of all the silly asses!'
And out into the street he ran
      To catch the speeding man.

Cried he: 'That quinine that you bought,
      (Since all may errors make),
I find was definitely not,—
      I sold you strychnine by mistake.
*Two* shillings is its price, and so
      Another bob you owe.'

# NAVELS

Men have navels more or less;
      Some are neat, some not.
Being fat I must confess
      Mine is far from hot.
Woman's is a pearly ring,
      Lovely to my mind;
So of it to shyly sing
      I am inclined.

I believe in nudity.
      Female forms divine
Should be bared for all to see
      In colour and in line.
So dear ladies, recognise
      The dimpling of your waist
Has approval in my eyes,
      Favour in my taste.

Darlings, please you, paint them gold,
      Or some pastel hue;
Make them starry to behold,
      Witching to the view.
Though I know I never should
      Say such things as this:
How a rosebud navel would
      Be sweet to kiss!

# MY CONSOLATION

'Nay; I don't need a hearing aid'
    I told Mama-in-law;
'For if I had I'd be afraid
    Of your eternal jaw;
Although at me you often shout,
    I'm undisturbed;
To tell the truth I can't make out
    A single word.'

And it's the same with others who
    Attempt to gab at me;
I listen to their point of view
    And solemnly agree.
To story stale and silly joke
    Stone deaf's my ear;
Each day a dozen stupid folk
    I fail to hear.

So silence that should be my grief
    Is my escape and shield;
From spiteful speech and base relief
    My aural sense is sealed.
And in my cosy cot of peace
    I close the door,
Praising the gods for rich relief
    From fool and bore.

# WILLIE

'Why did the lady in the lift
    Slap that poor parson's face?'
Said Mother, thinking as she sniffed,
    Of clerical disgrace.

Said Sonny Boy: 'Alas, I know.
    My conscience doth accuse me;
The lady stood upon my toe,
    Yet did not say—"Excuse me!"

'She hurt—and in that crowd confined
    I scarcely could endure it;
So when I pinched her fat behind
    She thought—it was the *Curate*.'

# BOXER'S WIFE

She phoned them when the Round was Eight:
    'How is my Joe?' they heard her say.
They answered: 'Gee! He's going great,
        Your guy's Okay.'

She phoned them when the Round was Nine:
    'How is my hero in the fray?'
They yelled: 'He leads; he's doing fine,—
        Joe's sure Okay.'

She phoned them when the Round was Ten:
    'Is it still Okay with my Joe?'
Reluctant came the answer then,—
        No Ma'am, KAYO.

# WHAT KISSES HAD JOHN KEATS?

I scanned two lines with some surmise
As over Keats I chanced to pore:
'And there I shut her wild, wild eyes
        With kisses four.'

Says I: 'Why was it only four,
Not five or six or seven?
I think I would have made it more,—
        Even eleven.

'Gee! If she'd lured a guy like me
Into her gelid grot
I'd make that Belle Dame sans Merci
        Sure kiss a lot.

'Them poets have their little tricks;
I think John counted kisses four,
Not two or three or five or six
        *To rhyme with "sore."*'

# THE CENTENARIAN

Great Grandfather was ninety-nine
      And so it was our one dread,
That though his health was superfine
      He'd fail to make the hundred.
Though he was not a rolling stone
      No moss he seemed to gather:
A patriarch of brawn and bone
        Was Great Grandfather.

He should have been senile and frail
      Instead of hale and hearty;
But no, he loved his mug of ale,
      A boisterous old party.
'As frisky as a colt,' said he,
      'A man's allotted span
I've lived but now I plan to be
      A Centenarian.'

Then one night when I called on him
      Oh what a change I saw!
His head was bowed, his eye was dim,
      Down-fallen was his jaw.
Said he: 'Leave me to die, I pray;
      I'm no more bloody use . . .
For in my mouth I found today—
      *A tooth that's loose.'*

# MY TAILS

I haven't worn my evening dress
    For nearly twenty years;
Oh I'm unsocial, I confess,
    A hermit, it appears.
So much moth-balled it's put away,
    And though wee wifie wails,
Never unto my dimmest day
      I'll don my tails.

How slim and trim I looked in them,
    Though I was sixty old;
And now their sleekness I condemn
    To lie in rigid fold.
I have a portrait of myself
    Proud-printed in the Press,
In garb now doomed to wardrobe shelf,—
    My evening dress.

So let this be my last request,
    That when I come to die,
In tails I may be deftly drest,
    With white waistcoat and tie.
No, not for me a vulgar shroud
    My carcass to caress;—
Oh let me do my coffin proud
    In evening dress!

# THE PRETTY LADY

He asked the lady in the train
If he might smoke: she smiled consent.
So lighting his cigar and fain
To talk he puffed away content,
Reflecting: how delightful are
        Fair dame and fine cigar.

Then from his bulging wallet he
A photograph with pride displayed,
His charming wife and children three,
When suddenly he was dismayed
To hear her say: 'These notes you've got,—
        I want the lot.'

He scarcely could believe his ears.
He laughed: 'The money isn't mine.
To pay it back would take me years,
And so politely I decline.
Madame, I think you speak in fun:
        Have you a gun?'

She smiled. 'No weapon have I got,
Only my virtue, but I swear
If you don't hand me out the lot
I'll rip my blouse, let down my hair,
Denounce you as a fiend accurst . . .''
        He told her: 'Do your worst.'

She did.  Her silken gown she tore,
Let down her locks and pulled the cord
That stopped the train, and from the floor
She greeted engineer and guard:
'I fought and fought in vain,' she cried.
　　　'Save me,—I'm terrified!'

The man was calm; he stood aloof.
Said he: 'Her game you understand;
But if you doubt, behold the proof
Of innocence is in my hand.'
And as they stared into the car
They saw his logic in a flash . . .
Aloft he held *a lit cigar*
　　　*With two inches of ash.*

# DERISIVE DITTIES

# GYPSY JILL

They're hanging Bill at eight o'clock,
     And millions will applaud.
He killed, and so they have to kill,
     Such is the will of God.
His brother Tom is on my bed
     To keep me comforted.

I see his bleary, blotchy face,
     I hear his sodden snore.
He plans that he can take Bill's place;
     I felt worse than a whore
As in his arms I cried all night,
     Thinking of poor Bill's plight.

I keep my eyes upon the clock;
     It nears the stroke of eight.
I think how bravely Bill will walk
     To meet his gallows fate . . .
His loaded gun is in the tent,—
     I know now what he meant.

Though Tom is boastful he will wed
        With me, no more to part,
I'll put a bullet through his head,
        Another through my heart:
At eight, stone-dead we three will be,
        —Bill, Tom and me.

# MY FEUD

I hate my neighbour Widow Green;
    I'd like to claw her face;
But if I did she'd make a scene
    And run me round the place:
For widows are in way of spleen
    A most pugnacious race.

And yet I must do something quick
    To keep the hag in line,
Since her red rooster chose to pick
    Five lettuce heads of mine:
And so I fed it arsenic
    Which it did not decline.

It disappeared, but on my mat
    Before a week had sped
I found Mi-mi, my tabby cat
    And it was stoney dead;
I diagnosed with weeping that
    On strychnine it had fed.

And so I bought a hamburg steak,
    Primed it with powdered glass,
And left it for her dog to take
    With gulping from the grass:
Since then, although I lie awake
    I have not seen it pass.

Well, that's the scoring up to date:
    And as I read a text
From Job to justify my hate
    I wonder who'll be next?
Somehow I feel that one must die,
    Ma Green or I.

# MARY ELLEN

It's mighty quiet in the house
    Since Mary Ellen quit me cold;
I've swept the hearth and fed the mouse
    That's getting fat and overbold.
I've bought a pig's foot for the pot
    And soon I'll set the fire alight;
Then I may eat or I may not,
    Depends upon my appetite.

Since Mary Ellen left me lone
    I haven't earned a bloody bob.
I sit and sigh, and mope and moan,
    And bellyache I quit my job.
My money's mostly gone,—I think
    I ought to save it up for food . . .
But no, I'll blow it in for drink,
    Then do a bunk for good.

I watch my mouse his whiskers preen;
    He watches me with wicked glee.
Today—oh God! It's years sixteen
    Since Mary Ellen wed with me.
Oh how the dear girl hated vermin!
    She left rat poison on the shelf . . .
Friend Mouse, your doom I now determine
    Then—how about myself?

# HENRY

Mary and I were twenty-two
    When we were wed;
A well-matched pair, right smart to view
    The town's folk said.
For twenty years I have been true
    To nuptial bed.

But oh alas! The march of time,
    Life's wear and tear!
Now I am in my lusty prime
    With pep to spare,
While she looks ten more years than I'm,
    With greying hair.

'Twas on our trip dear friends among,
    To New Orleans,
A stranger's silly trip of tongue
    Kiboshed my dreams:
I heard her say: 'How very young
    His *mother* seems.'

Child-bearing gets a woman down,
    And six had she;
Yet now somehow I feel a clown
    When she's with me;
When cuties smile one cannot frown,
    You must agree.

126

How often I have heard it said:
       'For happy fate,
In age a girl ten years ahead
       Should choose her mate.'
Now twenty years to Mary wed
       I know too late.

# BANK ROBBER

I much admire, I must admit,
        The man who robs a Bank;
It takes a lot of guts and grit,
        For lack of which I thank
The gods: a chap 'twould make of me
        You wouldn't ask to tea.

I do not mean a burglar cove
        Who climbs into a house,
From room to room flash-lit to rove
        As quiet as a mouse;
Ah no, in Crime he cannot rank
        With him who robs a Bank.

Who seemeth not to care a whoop
        For danger at its height;
Who handles what is known as 'soup,'
        And dandles dynamite:
Unto a bloke who can do that
        I doff my bowler hat.

I think he is the kind of stuff
        To be a mighty man
In battlefield,—aye, brave enough
        The Cross Victorian
To win and rise to high command,
        A hero in the land.

What General with all his swank
Has guts enough to rob a Bank!

# THE BANDIT

Upon his way to rob a Bank
      He paused to watch a fire;
Though crowds were pressing rank on rank
      He pushed a passage nigher;
Then sudden heard, piercing and wild,
      The screaming of a child.

A Public Enemy was he,
      A hater of the law;
He looked around for bravery
      But only fear he saw;
Then to the craven crowds amaze
      He plunged into the blaze.

How anguished was the waiting spell
      Of horror and of pain!
Then—then from out that fiery hell
      He staggered forth again:
The babe was safe, in blankets wrapt,
      The man flame lapt.

His record was an evil one,
      Of violence and sin.
No good on earth he'd ever done,
      Yet—may he Heaven win!
A gangster he . . . Is it not odd?
      —With guts of God.

# SENSITIVE BURGLAR

Selecting in the dining-room
       The silver of his choice,
The burglar heard from chamber gloom
       A female voice.
As cold and bitter as a toad,
       She spat a nasty name,
So even as his swag he stowed
       He blushed for shame.

'You dirty dog!' he heard her say,
       'I sniff your whisky stench.
I bet you've gambled half your pay,
       Or blown it on a wench.
Begone from here, you rakehell boor!
       You shame the human race.
What wife would pillow-share with your
       Disgusting face!'

A tear the tender burglar shed,
       Then indignation rose,
And swiftly striding to her bed
       He said: 'I'm none of those.
I am a connoisseur in crime
       And felonies I plan . . .
But otherwise, believe me I'm
       A GENTLEMAN.'

# THE PRISONER

Upspoke the culprit at the bar,
  Conducting his own case:
'Your Lordship, I have gone too far,
  But grant of me your grace.
As I was passing by a shop
  I saw my arm go out,
And though I begged of it to stop,
  It *stole* beyond a doubt.

'But why should my whole body be
  Condemned to dungeon grim,
For what in fact was only the
  Transgression of a limb?
So here before the Court I stand,
  And beg in Justice' name:
Please penalise my arm and hand,
  But not my frame.'

Outspoke the Judge with voice of ice,
  Although a smile he hid:
'Quite right!  You should not pay the price
  For what one member did.
Your reasoning I must admit;
  Your arm should gaol expect . . .
Three months!  And if you follow it
  The Court does not object.'

The culprit smiled with sudden charm,
Then to the Court's dismay,
Quickly removed a wooden arm
And went away.

# GENTLE GAOLER

Being a gaoler I'm supposed
    To be a hard-boiled guy;
Yet never prison walls enclosed
    A kinder soul than I:
Passing my charges precious pills
    To end their ills.

And if in gentle sleep they die,
    And pass to pleasant peace,
No one suspects that it is I
    Who gave them their release:
No matter what the Doctor thinks,
    The Warden winks.

A lifer's is a fearful fate;
    It wrings the heart of me.
And what a saving to the State
    A sudden death must be!
Doomed men should have the legal right
    To end their plight.

And so my veronel they take,
    And bid goodbye to pain;
And sleep, and never, never wake
    To living hell again:
Oh call me curst or call me blest,—
    I give them rest.

# GANGRENE

So often in the mid of night
      I wake me in my bed
With utter panic of affright
      To find my feet are dead;
And pace the floor to easy my pain
      And make them live again.

The folks at home are so discreet;
      They see me walk and walk
To keep the blood-flow in my feet,
      And though they never talk
I've heard them whisper: 'Mother may
      Have them *cut off* some day.'

Cut off my feet! I'd rather die . . .
      And yet the years of pain,
When in the darkness I will lie
      And pray to God in vain,
Thinking in agony: Oh why
Can doctors not annul our breath
      In honourable death?

# THE AFFLICTED

Softly every night they come
  To the picture show,
That old couple, *deaf and dumb*
  In the second row;
Wistful watching, hand in hand,
  Proud they understand.

Shut-ins from the world away,
  All in all to each;
Knowing utter joy as they
  Read the lips of speech . . .
Would, I wonder, I be glum
  Were I deaf and dumb?

Were I quieted away,
  Far from din and shock?
Were I spared the need to say
  Silly things in talk?
Utter hush I would not mind . . .
  Happy they!—I'm *blind*.

# POOR KID

Mumsie and Dad are raven dark
      And I am lily blonde.
' 'Tis strange,' I once heard nurse remark,
      'You do not correspond.'
And yet they claim me as their own,
      Born of their flesh and bone.

To doubt their parenthood I dread,
      But now to girlhood grown,
The thought is haunting in my head
      That I am *not* their own:
If so, my radiant bloom of youth
      Would wither in the truth.

'Twould give me anguish deep to know
      A fondling babe was I;
And that a maid in wedless woe
      Left me to live or die:
I'd rather Mother lied and lied
      To save my pride.

I love them both and they love me;
      I am their all, they say.
Yet though the sweetest home have we,
      To know I'm *theirs* I pray.
If not, please dear ones, never tell . . .
      The truth would be of hell.

# CONFETTI IN THE WIND

He wrote a letter in his mind
    To answer one a maid had sent;
He sought the fitting word to find,
    As on by hill and rill he went.
By bluebell wood and hawthorn lane,
    The cadence sweet and silken phrase
He incubated in his brain
    For days and days.

He wrote his letter on a page
    Of paper with a satin grain;
It did not ring, so in a rage
    He tore it up and tried again.
Time after time he drafted it;
    He polished it all through the night;
He tuned and pruned till bit by bit
    He got it right.

He took his letter to the post,
    Yet long he held it in his hand.
Strangely his mood had veered, almost
    Reversed,—he could not understand.
The girl was vague, the words were vain;
    April romance had come to grief . . .
He tore his letter up again,—
    Oh blest relief!

# THE CONTRAST

Fat lady, in your four-wheeled chair,
      Dolled up to beat the band,
At me you arrogantly stare
      With gold lorgnette in hand.
Oh how you differ from the dame
      So shabby, gaunt and grey,
With legs rheumatically lame,
      Who steers you on your way.

Nay, jewelled lady, look not back
      Lest you should be disturbed
To see the skinny hag in black
      Who boosts you up the curb.
Of course I know you get her cheap,
      Since she's a lady too,
And bite to eat and bed to sleep
      Maybe are all her due.

Alas for those who give us aid
      Yet need more help than we!
And though she thinks the wages paid
      Are almost charity,
I'd love to see that lady fat
      Lug round that hefty chair,
While with lorgnette and feathered hat
      Her handmaid lounges there.

# BIRD WATCHER

In Wall Street once a potent power,
 And now a multi-millionaire
Alone within a shady bower
 In clothes his valet would not wear,
He watches bird wings bright the air.

The man who mighty mergers planned,
 And oil and coal kinglike controlled,
With field-glasses in failing hand
 Spies downy nestlings five days old,
With joy he could not buy for gold.

Aye, even childlike is his glee;
 But how he crisps with hate and dread
And shakes a clawlike fist to see
 A kestrel hover overhead:
Though he would never shoot it dead.

Although his cook afar doth forage
 For food to woo his appetite,
The old man lives on milk and porridge
 And now it is his last delight
At eve if one lone linnet lingers
 To pick crushed almonds from his fingers.

# MY ANCESTORS

A barefoot boy I went to school
      To save a cobbler's fee,
For though the porridge pot was full
      A frugal folk were we;
We baked our bannocks, spun our wool,
      And counted each bawbee.

We reft our living from the soil,
      And I was shieling bred;
My father's hands were warped with toil,
      And crooked with grace he said.
My mother made the kettle boil
      As spinning wheel she fed.

My granny smoked a pipe of clay,
      And yammered of her youth;
The hairs upon her chin were grey,
      She had a single tooth;
Her mutch was grimed, I grieve to say,
      For I would speak the truth.

You of your ancestry may boast,—
        Well, here I brag of mine;
For if there is a heaven host
        I hope they'll be in line:
My dad with collie at his heel
        In plaid of tartan stripe;
My mammie with her spinning wheel,
        My granny with her pipe.

# LONGEVITY

Said Brown: 'I can't afford to die
    For I have bought annuity,
And every day of living I
    Have money coming in to me:
While others toil to make their bread
    I make mine by not being dead.'

Said Jones: 'I can't afford to die,
    For I have books and books to write.
I do not care for pelf but I
    Would versify my visions bright;
Emotions noble in my breast
    By worthy words should be expressed.'

Said Smith: 'I can't afford to die,
    Because my life is kindly planned;
So many on my care rely,
    For comfort and a helping hand.
Too many weak ones need me so,
    And will be woeful when I go.'

Then Death appraisingly looked down,
    Saying: 'Your time's up, Mister Brown.
And I am sorry, Mister Jones,
    The earth is ready for your bones.
Friend Smith, although you're overdue
    Your lease of living we'll renew . . .
Both fame and fortune far above,
    What matters in the end is—Love.'

# CAREERS

I knew three sisters,—all were sweet;
      Wishful to wed was I,
And wondered which would mostly meet
      The matrimonial tie.
I asked the first what fate would she
      Wish joy of life to bring her.
She answered: 'I would like to be
      A concert singer.'

I asked the second, for my mind
      Was set on nuptial noosing,
Unto what lot was she inclined
      If she could have the choosing?
Said she: 'For woman I can see
      No fortune finer,
Than to go in for Art and be
      A dress designer.'

With heavy heart I asked the third
      What was her life ambition;
A maiden she in look and word
      Of modest disposition.
'Alas, I dearly wish,' said she,
      'My aims were deeper:
My highest hope it is to be
      A good house-keeper.'

Which did I choose?  Look at my home,—
      The answer's there;
As neat and sweet as honeycomb,
      With children fair.
And so it humbly seems to me,
      In common life,
A woman's glory is to be
      A good house-wife.

# THE DECISION

Said she: 'Although my husband Jim
    Is with his home content,
I never should have married him,
    We are so different.
Oh yes, I know he loves me well,
    Our children he adores;
But he's so dull, and I rebel
    Against a life that bores.

'Of course there is another man,
    Quite pennyless is he;
And yet with hope and joy we plan
    A home beyond the sea.
Though I forfeit the name of wife
    And neighbours ostracise,
Such happiness will crown our life
    Their censure we'll despise.

'But then what will my children think,
    Whose love is pure and true?'
Said I: 'Your memory will stink
    If they should speak of you.
Your doting Jim will curse your name,
    And if you make a mess
Of life, oh do not in your shame
    Dare hope for happiness.'

Well, still with Jim she lives serene,
    And has of kiddies three.
'Oh what a fool I might have been
    To leave my home,' says she.
'Of course Jim is a priceless bore,
    But he's so sweet to me . . .
Come darling, won't you let me pour
    Another cup of tea?'

# SPARTAN MOTHER

My mother loved her horses and
        Her hounds of pedigree;
She did not kiss the baby hand
        I held to her in glee.
Of course I had a sweet *nou-nou*
        Who tended me with care,
And mother reined her nag to view
        Me with a critic air.

So I went to a famous school,
        But holidays were short;
My mother thought me just a fool,
        Unfit for games and sport.
For I was fond of books and art,
        And hated hound and steed:
Said Mother, 'Boy, you break my heart!
        You are not of our breed.'

Then came the War. The Mater said:
        'Thank God, a son I give
To King and Country,'—well, I'm *dead*
        Who would have loved to live.
'For England's sake,' said she, 'he died.
        For that my boy I bore.'
And now she talks of me with pride,
        A hero of the War.

Mother, I think that you are glad
        I ended up that way.
Your horses and your dogs you had,
        And still you have today.
Your only child you say *you* gave
        Your Country to defend . . .
Dear Mother, from a hero's grave
        I—curse you in the end.

# AT THE GOLDEN PIG

Where once with lads I scoffed my beer
 The landlord's lass I've wed.
Now I am lord and master here;—
 Thank God! the old man's dead.
I stand behind a blooming bar
 With belly like a tub,
And pals say, seeing my cigar:
  'Bill's wed a pub.'

I wonder now if I did well,
 My freedom for to lose;
Knowing my wife is fly as hell
 I mind my 'Ps' and 'Qs'.
Oh what a fuss she made because
 I tweaked the barmaid's bub:
Alas! a sorry day it was
  I wed a pub.

Fat landlord of the Golden Pig,
 They call me 'mister' now;
And many a mug of beer I swig,
 Yet don't get gay, somehow.
So farmer fellows, lean and clean
 Who sweat to earn your grub,
Although you haven't got a bean:
  *Don't wed a pub.*

# FLORRIE

Because I was a wanton wild
    And welcomed many a lover,
Who is the father of my child
    I wish I could discover.
For though I know it is not right
    In tender arms to tarry,
A barmaid has to be polite
    To Tom and Dick and Harry.

My truest love was Poacher Jim:
    I wish my babe was his'n.
Yet I can't father it on him
    Because he was in prison.
As uniforms I like, I had
    A soldier and a sailor;
Then there was Pete the painter lad,
    And Timothy the tailor.

Though virtue hurt you vice ain't nice;
    They say to err is human;
Alas! one pays a bitter price,
    It's hell to be a woman.
Oh dear!  Why was I born a lass
    Who hated to say: No, sir.
I'd better in my sorry pass
    Blame Mister Simms, the grocer.

# HORATIO

His portrait hung upon the wall.
  Oh how at us he used to stare.
Each Sunday when I made my call! —
  And when one day it wasn't there,
Quite quick I seemed to understand
  The light was green to hold her hand.

Her eyes were amorously lit;
  I knew she wouldn't mind at all.
Yet what I did was sit and sit
  Seeing that blankness on the wall . . .
Horatio had a gentle face,—
  How would my mug look in his place?

That oblong of wall-paper wan!
  And while she prattled prettily
I sensed the *red* light going on,
  So I refused a cup of tea,
And took my gold-topped cane and hat—
  My going seemed to leave her flat.

Horatio was a decent guy,
    And when she ravished from her heart
A damsite better man than I,
    She seemed to me,—well, just a tart:
Her lack of tact I can't explain.
    His picture,—is it hung again?

# RHYMES FOR RESIGNATION

# CLEMENCEAU

His frown brought terror to his foes,
    But now in twilight of his days
The pure perfection of a rose
    Can kindle rapture in his gaze.
Where once he swung the sword of wrath
    And peoples trembled at his word,
With hoe he trims a pansied path
        And listens to a bird.

His large of life was lived with noise,
    With war and strife and crash of kings:
But now he hungers for the joys
    Of peace, and hush of homely things.
His old dog nuzzles by his knee,
    And seems to say: 'Oh Master dear,
Please do not ever part from me!
        We are so happy here.'

His ancient maid, as sky draws dim,
    Calls to him that the soup grows cold.
She tyrannises over him
    Who once held armies in his hold.
With slippers, old skull-cap and shawl
    He dreams and dozes by the fire,
Sighing: 'Behold the end of all,
        Sweet rest my sole desire.

'My task is done, my pen is still;
    My Book is there for all to see,—
The final triumph of my will,
    Ineffably, my victory.
A Tiger once, but now a lamb,
    With frailing hand my gate I close.
How hushed my heart! My life how calm!
      —Its crown a Rose.'

# MISTINGUETTE

He was my one and only love;
My world was mirror for his face.
We were as close as hand and glove,
Until he came with smiling grace
To say: 'We must be wise, my dear.
You are the idol of today,
But I too plan a proud career,—
Let's kiss and go our way.'

And then he soared to sudden fame,
And even queens applauded him.
A halo glorified his name
That dust of time may never dim.
And me,—I toured golden Brazil,
Yet as gay mobs were cheering me,
The sun seemed black, the brilliance chill,
My triumph mockery.

Today if I should say: 'Hello!'
He'd say: 'How are you?' I'd say: 'Fine.'
Yet never shall he see the woe,
The wanness of my frail decline.
I love him now and always will.
Oh may his star be long to set!
My Maurice is an idol still,—
What wreaths for Mistinguette!

# ERNIE PYLE

I wish I had the simple style
      In writing verse,
As in his prose had Ernie Pyle,
      So true and terse;
Springing so forthright from the heart
      With guileless art.

I wish I could put back a dram
      As Ernie could;
I wish that I could cuss and damn
      As soldier should;
And fain with every verse would I
      Ernie outvie.

Alas! I cannot claim his high
      Humanity;
Nor emulate his pungent, dry
      Profanity;
Nor share his love of common folk
      Who bear life's yolk.

Oh Ernie, who on earth I knew
      In war and wine,
Though frail of frame, in soul how you
      Were pure and fine!
I'm proud that once when we were plastered
      You called me 'bastard.'

# EINSTEIN

A little mousey man he was
    With board, and chalk in hand;
And millions were awestruck because
    They couldn't understand.
Said he: 'E equals Mc 2:
        I'll prove it true.'

No doubt you can, your marvel man,
    But will it serve our good?
Will it prolong our living span
    And multiply our food?
Will it bring peace between the nations
        To make equations?

Our thanks are due no doubt to you
    For truth beyond our ken;
But after all what did you do
    To ease the lot of men?
How can a thousand 'yous' be priced
        Beside a Christ?

# TOM PAINE

An Englishman was Thomas Paine
       Who bled for liberty;
But while his fight was far from vain
       He died in poverty:
Though some are of the sober thinking
       'Twas due to drinking.

Yet this is what appeals to me:
       Cobbet, a friend, loved him so well
He sailed across the surly sea
       To raw and rigid New Rochelle:
With none to say: 'Take him not from us!'
       He raped the grave of Thomas.

And in his library he set
       These bones so woe-begone;
I have no doubt his eyes were wet
       To scan that skeleton.
That grinning scull from which in season
       Emerged the *Age of Reason*.

Then Cobbet in his turn lay dead,
       And auctioneering tones
Over his chattels rudely said:
       'Who wants them bloody bones?'
None did, so they were scattered far
       And God knows where they are.

164

A friend of Franklin and of Pitt
       He lived a stormy span;
The flame of liberty he lit
       And rang the Rights of Man.
Yet pilgrims from Vermont and Maine
In hero worship seek in vain
       The bones of Thomas Paine.

# DYLAN

And is it not a gesture grand
  To drink oneself to death?
Oh sure 'tis I can understand,
  Being of sober breath.
And so I do not sing success,
  But dirge the damned who fall,
And who contempt for life express
   Through alcohol.

Of Stephen Foster and of Poe,
  Of Burns and Wilde I think;
And weary men who dared to go
  The wanton way of drink.
Strange mortals blind to bitter blame,
  And deaf to loud delight,
Who from the shades of sin and shame
   Enstar our night.

Among those dupes of destiny
  Add D.T. to my list,
Although his verse you may agree
  Leaves one in mental mist . . .
Oh ye mad poets, loth of life,
  Who peace in death divine,
Pass not by pistol, poison, knife,—
   Drown, drown in wine!

# A CANVAS FOR A CRUST

Aye, Montecelli, that's the name.
You may have heard of him perhaps.
Yet though he never savoured fame,
Of those impressionistic chaps,
Monet and Manet and Renoir
              He was the avatar.

He festered in a Marseilles slum,
A starving genius, god-inspired.
You'd take him for a lousy bum,
Tho' poetry of paint he lyred,
In dreamy pastels each a gem: . . .
              How people laughed at them!

He peddled paint from bar to bar;
From sordid rags a jewel shone,
A glow of joy and colour far
From filth of fortune woe-begone.
'Just twenty francs,' he shyly said,
              'To take me drunk to bed.'

Of Van Gogh and Cezanne a peer;
In dreams of ecstasy enskied,
A genius and a pioneer,
Poor, paralysed and mad he died:
Yet by all who hold Beauty dear
              May he be glorified!

# BENJAMIN FRANKLIN

Franklin fathered bastards fourteen,
    (So I read in the *New Yorker*);
If it's true, in terms of courtin'
    Benny must have been a corker.
To be prudent I've aspired,
    And my passions I have mastered;
So that I have never sired
        A single bastard.

One of course can never know;
    But I think that if I had
It would give me quite a glow
    When a kiddie called me 'Dad.'
Watching toddlers at their play,
    Parentage I'd gladly claim,
But their mothers smiling say:
        'You're not to blame.'

Ben founded the *Satevepost,*
    And for that I much respect him;
But fourteen is quite a host
    Paternally to elect him.
'Fatherhood is not a crime,'
    Deemed fat Ben, 'there *could* be others . . .
Darlings, I had not the time
        To wed your mothers.'

# THE SEED

I was a seed that fell
    In silver dew;
And nobody could tell,
    For no one knew;
No one could tell my fate,
    As I grew tall;
None visioned me with hate,
    No, none at all.

A sapling I became,
    Blest by the sun;
No rumour of my shame
    Had any one.
Oh I was proud indeed,
    And sang with glee,
When from a tiny seed
    I grew a tree.

I was so stout and strong
    Though still so young,
When sudden came a throng
    With angry tongue;
They cleft me to the core
    With savage blows,
And from their ranks a roar
    Of rage arose.

I was so proud a seed
     A tree to grow;
Surely there was no need
     To lay me low.
Why did I end so ill,
     The midst of three
Black crosses on a hill
     Called Calvary?

# STUPIDITY

*Stupidity,* woe's anodyne,
Be kind and comfort me in mine;
Smooth out the furrows of my brow,
Make me as carefree as a cow,
Content to sleep and eat and drink
                    And never think.

*Stupidity,* let me be blind
To all the ills of humankind;
Fill me with simple sentiment
To walk the way my father went;
School me to sweat with robot folk
                    Beneath the yoke.

*Stupidity,* keep in their place
The moiling masses of my race,
And bid the lowly multitude
Be humble as a people should;
Learn us with patient hearts, I pray,
                    Lords to obey.

*Stupidity* and Ignorance,
Be you our buffers 'mid mischance;
Endoctrine us to do your will,
And other stupid people kill;
Fool us with hope of Life to be,
Great god to whom we bow the knee,
　　　　—STUPIDITY.

# THE AFTERMATH

Although my blood I've shed
     In war's red wrath,
Oh how I darkly dread
     Its aftermath!
Oh how I fear the day
     Of my release,
When I must face the fray
     Of phoney peace!

When I must fend again
     In labour strife;
And toil with sweat and strain
     For kids and wife.
The world is so upset
     I battled for,
That grimly I regret
     The peace of war.

The wounds are hard to heal
     Of shell and shard,
But O the way to weal
     Is bitter hard!
Though looking back I see
     A gory path,
How bloody black can be
     War's Aftermath!

# LITTLE BROTHER

Wars have been and wars will be
Till the human race is run;
Battles red by land and sea,
Never peace beneath the sun.
I am old and little care;
I'll be cold, my lips be dumb:
Brother mine, beware, beware . . .
Evil looms the wrath to come.

Eastern skies are dark with strife,
Western lands are stark with fear;
Rumours of world-war are rife,
Armageddon draweth near.
If your carcase you would save,
Hear, oh hear, the dreadful drum!
Fly to forest, cower in cave . . .
Brother, heed the wrath to come!

Brother, you were born too late;
Human life is but a breath.
Men delve deep, where darkly wait
Sinister the seeds of death,
There's no moment to delay;
Sorrowing the stars are blind.
Little Brother, how I pray
You may sanctuary find.
Peoples of the world succumb . . .
Fly, poor fools, the WRATH TO COME!

# AT THE PARADE

I cannot flap a flag
　　　Or beat a drum;
Behind the mob I lag
　　　With larynx dumb;
Alas! I fear I'm not
　　　A Patriot.

With acrid eyes I see
　　　The soul of things;
And equal unto me
　　　Are cooks and kings;
I would not cross the street
　　　A duke to meet.

Oh curse me for a fool
　　　To be so proud;
To stand so still and cool
　　　Amid the crowd.
For President or Peer
　　　God, let me cheer!

But no, despite the glee
　　　My heart is cold;
I think that it may be
　　　Because I'm old;
I'm dumb where millions yell . . .
　　　*Oh what the hell!*

# COMPASSION

What puts me in a rage is
The sight of cursed cages
Where singers of the sky
Perch hop instead of fly;
Where lions to and fro
Pace seven yards or so:
I who love space of stars
Have hate of bars.

I wince to see dogs chained,
Or horses bit restrained;
Or men of feeble mind
In straight-jackets confined;
Or convicts in black cells
Enduring earthly hells:
To me not to be free
Is fiendish cruelty.

To me not to be kind
Is evil of the mind.
No need to pray or preach,
Let us our children teach
With every fond caress
Pity and gentleness:
So in the end may we
God's Kingdom bring to be.

# MY ROOM

I think the things I own and love
        Acquire a sense of me,
That gives them value far above
        The worth that others see.
My chattels are of me a part:
        This chair on which I sit
Would break its overstuffed old heart
        If I made junk of it.

To humble needs with which I live,
        My books, my desk, my bed,
A personality I give
        They'll lose when I am dead.
Sometimes on entering my room
        They look at me with fear,
As if they had a sense of doom
        Inevitably near.

Yet haply, since they do not die,
        In them will linger on
Some of the spirit that was I,
        When I am gone.
And maybe some sweet soul will sigh,
        And stroke with tender touch
The things I loved, and even cry
        A little,—not too much.

# SAILOR SON

When you come home I'll not be round
   To welcome you.
They'll take you to a grassy mound
   So neat and new;
Where I'll be sleeping—O so sound!
   The ages through.

I'll not be round to broom the hearth,
   To feed the chicks;
And in the wee room of your birth
   Your bed to fix;
Rose room that knew your baby mirth
   Your tiny tricks.

I'll not be round . . . The garden still
   With bees will hum;
To cheerful you the throstle's bill
   Will not be dumb;
The rambler rose will overspill
   When you will come.

Bird, bee and bloom, they'll greet you all
   With scented sound;
Yet though the joy of your footfall
   Will thrill the ground
Your mother with her old grey shawl—
   Will not be round.

# DEDICATION

In youth I longed to paint
    The loveliness I saw;
And yet by dire constraint
    I had to study Law.
But now all that is past,
    And I have no regret,
For I am free at last
    Law to forget.

To beauty newly born
    With brush and tube I play;
And though my daubs you scorn,
    I'll learn to paint some day.
When I am eighty old,
    Maybe I'll better them,
And you may yet behold
    A gem.

Old Renoir used to paint,
    Brush strapped to palsied hand;
His fervour of a saint
    How I can understand.
My joy is my reward,
    And though you gently smile,
Grant me to fumble, Lord,
    A little while!

# TICK-TOCK

Tick-tocking in my ear
My dollar clock I hear.
'Arise,' it seems to say:
'Behold another day
To grasp the golden key
Of Opportunity;
To turn the magic lock—
   Tick-tock!

'Another day to gain
Some goal you sought in vain;
To sing a sweeter song,
Perchance to right a wrong;
To win a height unscaled
Where yesterday you failed;
To brave a battle shock—
   Tick-tock!'

You measure out my breath,
Each beat one nearer death . . .
O God, grant unto me
A few more years to be,
That somehow I may prove
My loyalty and love:
Wind up this worn-out clock,
   Tick-tock,
   Tick-tock!

# AT EIGHTY YEARS

As nothingness draws near
       How I can see
Inexorably clear
       My vanity.
My sum of worthiness
       Always so small,
Dwindles from less to less
       To none at all.

As grisly destiny
       Claims me at last,
How grievous seem to me
       Sins of my past!
How keen a conscience edge
       Can come to be!
How pitiless the dredge
       Of memory!

Ye proud ones of the earth
       Who count your gains,
What cherish you of worth
       For all your pains?
E'er death shall slam the door,
       Will you, like me,
Face fate and count the score—
       FUTILITY.

# SEVEN

If on water and sweet bread
Seven years I'll add to life,
For me will no blood be shed,
No lamb know the evil knife;
Excellently will I dine
On a crust and Adam's wine.

If a bed in monkish cell
Will mean old of age to me,
Let me in a convent dwell,
And from fellow men be free;
Let my mellow sunset days
Pass in piety and praise.

For I love each hour I live,
Wishing it were twice as long;
Dawn my gratitude I give,
Laud the Lord with evensong:
Now that moons are sadly few
How I grudge the grave its due!

Yet somehow I seem to know
Seven Springs are left to me;
Seven Mays may cherry tree
Will allume with sudden snow . . .
Then let seven candles shine
Silver peace above my shrine.

# SEA SORCERY

Oh how I love the laughing sea,
    Sun lances splintering;
Or with a virile harmony
    In salty caves to sing;
Or mumbling pebbles on the shore,
    Or roused to monster might:
By day I love the sea, but more
    I love it in the night.

High over ocean hangs my home
    And when the moon is clear
I stare and stare till fairy foam
    Is music in my ear;
Till glamour dances to a tune
    No mortal man could make;
And there bewitched beneath the moon
    To beauty I awake.

Then though I seek my bed again
    And close the shutters tight,
Still, still I hear that wild refrain
    And see that mystic light . . .
Oh reckon me a crazy loon,
    But blessèd I will be
If my last seeing be the moon,
    My last sound—the Sea.

# O LOVELY LIE

I told a truth, a tragic truth
      That tore the sullen sky;
A million shuddered at my sooth
      And anarchist was I.
Red righteousness was in my word
      To winnow evil chaff;
Yet while I swung crusading sword
      I heard the devil laugh.

I framed a lie, a rainbow lie
      To glorify a thought;
And none was so surprise as I
      When fast as fire it caught.
Like honey people lapped my lie
      And peddled it abroad,
Till in a lift of sunny sky
      I saw the smile of God.

If falsehood may be best, I thought,
      To hell with verity;
Dark truth may be a cancer spot
      'Twere better not to see.
Aye, let a lie be big and bold
      Yet ripe with hope and ruth,
Beshrew me! but its heart may hold
      More virtue than the truth.

# THE PALACE

Grimy men with picks and shovels
    Who in darkness sweat unseen,
Climb from out your lousy hovels,
    Build a palace for the Queen;
Praise the powers that be for giving
    You a chance to make a living.

Yet it would be better far
    Could you build with cosy lure
Skyey tenements where are
    Rabbit-warrens of the poor;
With a hope bright as a gem
    Some day you might live in them.

Could the Queen just say: 'A score
    Of rich palaces have I.
Do not make me any more,—
    Raise a hostel heaven-high;
House the hundreds who have need,
    To their misery give heed.'

Could she make this gesture fine
    To the pit where labour grovels,
Mother hearts would cease to pine,
    Weary men would wave their shovels.
All would cry with hope serene:
    'Little children, bless the Queen!'

# ORPHAN SCHOOL

Full fifty merry maids I heard
>           One summer morn a-singing;
And each was like a joyous bird
>           With spring-clear note a-ringing.
It was an old-time soldier song
>           That held their happy voices:
Oh how it's good to swing along
>                When youth rejoices!

Then lo! I dreamed long years had gone,
>           They passed again ungladly.
Their backs were bent, their cheeks were wan,
>           Their eyes were staring sadly.
Their ranks were thinned by full a score
>           From death's remorseless reaping;
Their steps were slow, they sang no more,—
>                Nay, some were weeping.

Dark dream! I saw my maids today
>           Singing so innocently;
Their eyes with happiness were gay,
>           They looked at me so gently.
Thought I: Be merry in your youth
>           With hearts unrueing:
Thank God you do not know the truth
>                Of Life's Undoing!

# JOEY

I thought I would go daft when Joey died.
He was my first, and wise beyond his years.
For nigh a hundred nights I cried and cried,
Until my weary eyes burned up my tears.
Willie and Rosie tried to comfort me:
A woeful, weeping family were we.

I was a widow with no friends at all,
Ironing men's shirts to buy my kiddies grub;
And then one day a lawyer came to call,
Me with my arms deep in the washing-tub.
The gentleman who ran poor Joey down
Was willing to give us a thousand poun'.

What a godsend! It meant goodbye to care,
The fear of being dumped out on the street.
Rosie and Willie could have wool to wear,
And more than bread and margerine to eat . . .
To Joey's broken little legs we owe
Our rescue from a fate of want and woe.

*How happily he hurried home to me,*
*Bringing a new-baked, crisp-brown loaf of bread.*
*The headlights of the car he did not see,*
*And when help came they thought that he was dead.*
*He stared with wonder from a face so wan . . .*
*A long, last look and he was gone,—was gone.*

We've comfort now, and yet it hurts to know
We owe our joy to little, laughing Joe.

*SONGS  FOR  SERENITY*

# SYMPATHY

My Muse is simple,—yet it's nice
To think you don't need to think twice
   On words I write.
I reckon I've a common touch
And if you say I cuss too much
   I answer: 'Quite!'

I envy not the poet's lot;
He has something I haven't got,
   Alas, I know.
But I have something maybe he
Would envy just a mite in me,—
   I'm rather *low*.

For I am cast of common clay,
And from a ditch I fought my way,
   And that is why
The while the poet scans the skies,
My gaze is grimly gutterwise,
   Earthy am I.

And yet I have a gift, perhaps
Denied to proud poetic chaps
         Who scoff at me;
I know the hearts of humble folk;
I too have bowed beneath the yoke:
So let my verse for them evoke
         Your sympathy.

# MY CHAPEL

In idle dream with pipe in hand
    I looked across the Square,
And saw the little chapel stand
    In eloquent despair.
A ruin of the War it was,
    A dreary, dingy mess:
It worried me a lot because
    My hobby's happiness.

The shabby Priest said: 'You are kind.
    Time leaves us on the lurch,
And there are very few who mind
    Their duty to the Church.
But with this precious sum you give,
    I'll make it like a gem;
Poor folks will come, our altar live
    To comfort them.'

So now my chapel of despair
    Is full of joy and song;
I watch the humble go to prayer
    Although I don't belong.
An artist and agnostic I
    Possess but little pelf;
But oh what blessings it can buy
    Them—and myself!

# THE GOAT AND I

Each sunny day upon my way
      A goat I pass;
He has a beard of silver grey,
      A bell of brass.
And all the while I am in sight
      He seems to muse,
And stares at me with all his might
      And chews and chews.

Upon the hill so thymy sweet
      With joy of Spring,
He hails me with a tiny bleat
      Of welcoming.
Though half the globe is drenched with blood
      And cities flare,
Contentedly he chews the cud
      And does not care.

Oh gentle friend, I know not what
      Your age may be,
But of my years I'd give the lot
      Yet left to me,
To chew a thistle and not choke,
      But bright of eye
Gaze at the old world-weary bloke
      Who hobbles by.

Alas! though bards make verse sublime,
          And lines to quote,
It takes a fool like me to rhyme
          About a goat.

# YOU AND ME

I'm part of people I have known
        And they are part of me;
The seeds of thought that I have sown
        In other minds I see.
There's something of me in the throne
        And in the gallows tree.

There's something of me in each one
        With whom I work and play,
For islanded there can be none
        In this dynamic day;
And meshed with me perchance may be
        A leper in Cathay.

There's me in you and you in me,
        For deeply in us delves
Such common thought that never we
        Can call ourselves ourselves.
In coils of universal fate
        No man is isolate.

For you and I are History,
        The all that ever was;
And woven in the tapestry
        Of everlasting laws,
Persist will we in Time to be,
        Forever you and me.

# PERIODS

My destiny it is tonight
    To sit with pensive brow
Beside my study fire and write
    This verse I'm making now.
This Period, this tiny dot
    My pencil has defined,
By centuries of human thought
       Was predestined.

And my last period of all
    With patience now I see;
The final point so very small,
    That locks my life for me.
Yet in eternity of time
    They relatively seem
So like,—the dot that rounds my rhyme
      Or ends my dream.

For each was preordained by Fate
    Since human life began;
So are the little and the great
    Linked in the life of man.
And as I wait without heartache
    The pencil-point of God,
To pattern predestined I make
      This——.

# WHEELS

Since I am sick of Wheels
   That jar my day,
Unto the hush that heals
   I steal away.
Unto the core of Peace
   Nature reveals,
I go to win release
   From Wheels.

Let me beneath the moon
   Take desert trail;
Or on some lost lagoon
   Serenely sail;
Win to some peak the grey
   Storm cloud conceals . . .
Life, let me get away
   From Wheels!

Why was I born so late?
   A skin-clad man
I should have shared the fate
   Of mountain clan;
My quiet flock beside,
   When silence steals,
Unshocked in eventide
   By Wheels.

The Wheel is King today,
      And speed's a god;
Yet when I see the way
      My feet have trod,
Like pilgrims who to shrine
      Of Beauty kneels,
I pray: O Peace divine
      *Damn Wheels!*

# MY HUNDRED BOOKS

A thousand books my library
    Contains;
And all are primed, it seems to me,
    With brains.
Mine are so few I scratch in thought
    My head;
For just a hundred of the lot
    I've read.

A hundred books, but of the best,
    I can
With wisdom savour and digest
    And scan.
Yet when afar from kin and kith
    In nooks
Of quietness I'm happy with
    Sweet books.

So as nine hundred at me stare
    In vain,
My lack I'm wistfully aware
    Of brain;
Yet as my leave of living ends,
    With looks
Of love I view a hundred friends,
    My Books.

# TWO WORDS

'God' is composed of letters three,
> But if you put an 'l'
Before the last it seems to me
> A synonym for Hell.
For all of envy, greed and hate
> The human heart can hold
Respond unto the devil's bait
> Of Gold.

When God created Gold to be
> For our adorning fit,
I little think he dreamed that we
> Would come to worship it.
But when you ruefully have scanned
> The chronicles of Time,
You'll find that lucre lends a hand
> To Crime.

So if you are a millionaire,
> To be of Heaven sure,
Give every penny you can spare
> Unto the sick and poor.
From Gold strike out the evil 'ell,'
> And so with letters odd
You can with peace of spirit spell
> Just GOD.

# THE CHOICE

Some inherit manly beauty,
Some come into worldly wealth;
Some have lofty sense of duty,
Others boast exultant health.
Though the pick may be confusing,
Health, wealth, charm or character,
If you had the chance of choosing
       Which would you prefer?

I'm not sold on body beauty,
Though health I appreciate;
Character and sense of duty
I resign to Men of State.
I don't need a heap of money;
Oh I know I'm hard to please.
Though to you it may seem funny,
       I want none of these.

No, give me Imagination,
And the gift of weaving words
Into patterns of creation,
With the lilt of singing birds;
Passion and the power to show it,
Sense of life with love expressed:
Let me be a bloody poet,—
       You can keep the rest.

# A MEDIOCRE MAN

I'm just a mediocre man
    Of no high-brow pretence;
A comfortable life I plan
    With care and commonsense.
I do the things most people do,
    I echo what they say;
And through my morning paper view
    The problems of the day.

No doubt you think I'm colourless,
    Profoundly commonplace;
And yet I fancy, more or less,
    I represent the race.
My name may stand for everyone,
    At least for nine in ten,
For all in all the world is run
    By mediocre men.

Of course you'll maybe not agree
    That *you* are average,
And unlike ordinary me
    You strut your little stage,
Well, you may even own a Bank,
    And mighty mergers plan,
But Brother, doff your tile and thank
    The Mediocre Man.

# IMAGINATION

A gaunt and hoary slab of stone
  I found in desert space,
And wondered why it lay alone
  In that abandoned place.
Said I: 'Maybe a Palace stood
  Where now the lizards crawl,
With courts of musky quietude
  And turrets tall.

Maybe where low the vultures wing
  'Mid mosque and minaret,
The proud pavilion of a King
  Was luminously set.
'Mid fairy fountains, alcoves dim,
  Upon a garnet throne
He ruled,—and now all trace of him
  Is just this stone.

Ah well, I've done with wandering,
  But from a blousy bar
I see with drunk imagining
  A Palace like a star.
I build it up from one grey stone
  With gardens hanging high,
And dream . . . Long, long ere Babylon
  Its King was I.

# TO A STUFFED SHIRT

On the tide you ride head high,
Like a whale 'mid little fishes;
I should envy you as I
Help my wife to wash the dishes.
Yet frock-coat and stove-pipe hat
Cannot hide your folds of fat.

You are reckoned a success,
And the public praise you win;
There's your picture in the Press,
Pouchy eyes and triple chin.
Wealth,—of it you fairly stink;
Health,—what does your Doctor think?

Dignity is phoney stuff.
Who is dignified deep down?
Strip the pants off, call the bluff,
Common clay are king and clown.
Let a bulging belly be
Your best bid for dignity.

Miserable millionaire!
For indulgence you must pay.
Yet there's salvation in prayer,—
Down on your fat knees and pray.
Know that with your dying breath
There is dignity in death.

# WORDS

If on isle of the sea
      I have to tarry,
With *one* book, let it be
      A Dictionary.
For though I love life's scene,
      It seems absurd,
My greatest joy has been
      The printed word.

Though painter with delight
      May colours blend,
They are but in his sight
      Means to an end.
Yet while I harmonise
      Or pattern them,
A precious word I prize
      Like to a gem.

A fiddler lures fine tone
      From gut and wood;
A sculptor from stark stone
      Shapes godlihood.
But let me just caress,
      Like silver birds,
For their own loveliness—
      Bewitching words.

# THE SEARCH

I bought a young and lovely bride,
   Paying her father gold;
Lamblike she rested by my side,
   As cold as ice is cold.
No love in her could I awake,
   Even for pity's sake.

I bought rich books I could not read,
   And pictures proud and rare;
Reproachfully they seemed to plead
   And hunger for my care;
But to their beauty I was blind,
   Even as is a hind.

The bearded merchants heard my cry:
   'I'll give all I possess
If only, only I can buy
   A little happiness.'
Alas! I sought without avail:
   They had not *that* for sale.

I gave my riches to the poor
   And dared the desert lone;
Now of God's heaven I am sure
   Though I am rag and bone . . .
Aye, richer than the Aga Khan,
   At last—a happy man.

# TOURISTS

In a strange town in a far land
   They met amid a throng;
They stared, they could not understand
   How life was sudden song.
As brown eyes looked in eyes of grey
   Just for a moment's space,
Twin spirits met with sweet dismay
   In that strange place.

And then the mob that swept them near
   Reft them away again;
Two hearts in all the world most dear
   Knew puzzlement and pain.
They barely brushed in passing by,
   A wildered girl and boy,
Who should have clasped with laughing cry,
   And wept for joy.

But no, the crowd cleft them apart,
   And she went East, he West;
But there was havoc in his heart
   And brooding in her breast.
In a far land, in a strange town
   Amid a mob they met;
They stared, they passed . . . But O deep down,
   Can they forget?

# THE ROBBERS

Alas! I see that thrushes three
　　Are ravishing my old fig tree,
In whose green shade I smoked my pipe
　　And waited for the fruit to ripe;
From green to purple softly swell
　　Then drop into my lap to tell
That it is succulently sweet
　　And excellent to eat.

And now I see the crimson streak,
　　The greedy gash of yellow beak.
And look! the finches come in throng,
　　In wavy passage, light with song;
Of course I could scare them away,
　　But with a shrug: 'The heck!' I say.
I owe them something for their glee,
　　So let them have their spree.

For all too soon in icy air
     My fig tree will be bleak and bare,
Until it wake from Winter sleep
     And button buds begin to peep.
Then broad leaves come to shelter me
     In luminous placidity.
Then figs will ripen with a rush
     And brash will come the thrush.

But what care I though birds destroy
My fruit,—they pay me back with joy.

# MY VINEYARD

To me at night the stars are vocal.
They say: 'Your planet's oh so local!
A speck of dust in heaven's ceiling;
Your faith divine a foolish feeling.
What odds if you are chaos hurled,
Yours is a silly little world.'

For their derision, haply true,
I hate the stars, as wouldn't you?
But whether earth be great or little,
I do not care a fishwife's spittle;
I do not fret its where or why,—
Today's a day and I am I.

Serene, afar from woe and worry
I tend my vines and do not hurry.
I buss the lass and tip the bottle,
Fill up the glass and rinse my throttle.
Tomorrow though the earth should perish,
The lust of life today I cherish.

Ah no, the stars I will not curse:
Though things are bad they might be worse.
So when vast constellations shine
I drink to them in ruby wine;
For they themselves,—although it odd is,
Somehow give me a sense that God is.

Because we trust and realise
His love he steers us in the skies.
For faith however foolish can
Be mighty helpful to a man:
And as I tend my vines so He
With tenderness looks after me.

# MY DOG'S MY BOSS

Each day when it's anighing three
        Old Dick looks at the clock,
Then proudly brings my stick to me
        To mind me of our walk.
And in his doggy rapture he
        Does everything but talk.

But since I lack his zip and zest
        My old bones often tire;
And so I ventured to suggest
        Today we hug the fire.
But with what wailing he expressed
        The death of his desire!

He gazed at me with eyes of woe
        As if to say: 'Old Boy,
You mustn't lose your grip, you know,
        Let us with laughing joy,
On heath and hill six miles or so
        Our legs and lungs employ.'

And then his bark stilled to a sigh
      He flopped upon the floor;
But such a soft old mug am I
      I threw awide the door;
So gaily, though the wind was high
      We hiked across the moor.

# BREATH IS ENOUGH

I draw sweet air
Deeply and long,
As pure as prayer,
As sweet as song.
Where lilies glow
And roses wreath,
Heart-joy I know
Is just to breathe.

Aye, so I think
By shore or sea,
As deep I drink
Of purity.
This brave machine,
Bare to the buff,
I keep ice-clean,
Breath is enough.

From mountain stream
To covert cool
The world, I deem,
Is wonderful;
The great, the small,
The smooth, the rough,
I love it all,—
Breath is enough.

# RIPENESS

With peace and rest
And wisdom sage,
Ripeness is best
Of every age.
With hands that fold
In pensive prayer,
For grave-yard mold
      Prepare.

From fighting free
With fear forgot,
Let ripeness be,
Before the rot.
With heart of cheer
At eighty odd,
How man grows near
      To God!

With passion spent
And life nigh run
Let us repent
The ill we've done.
And as we bless
With happy heart
Life's mellowness
     —Depart.

# A CABBAGE PATCH

Folk ask if I'm alive,
        Most think I'm not;
Yet gaily I contrive
        To till my plot.
The world its way can go,
        I little heed,
So long as I can grow
        The grub I need.

For though long overdue,
        The years to me,
Have taught a lesson true,
        —Humility.
Such better men than I
        I've seen pass on;
Their pay-off when they die:
        —Oblivion.

And so I mock at fame,
        With books unread;
No monument I claim
        When I am dead;
Contented as I see
        My cottage thatch
That my last goal should be
        —A cabbage patch.

# THE SCORE

I asked a silver sage
  With race nigh run:
'Tell me in old of age
  Your wisdom won?'
Said he: 'From fret and strife
  And vain vexation,
The all I've learned from life
  Is—Resignation.'

I asked a Bard who thrummed
  A harp clay-cold:
'How is your story summed
  Now you are old?'
Though golden voice was his,
  And fame had he,
He sighed: 'The finish is
  —Futility.'

I'm old; I have no wealth
  Toil to reward;
Yet for the boon of health
  I thank the Lord.
While Beauty I can see,
  To *live* is good;
And so life's crown to me
  Is—Gratitude.

# WORK AND JOY

Each day I live I thank the Lord
        I do the work I love;
And in it find a rich reward,
        All price and praise above.
For few may do the work they love,
        The fond unique employ,
That fits them as a hand a glove,
        And gives them joy.

Oh gentlefolk, do you and you
        Who toil for daily hire,
Consider that the job you do
        Is to your heart's desire?
Aye, though you are to it resigned,
        And will no duty shirk,
Oh do you in your private mind
        *Adore* your work?

Twice happy man whose job is joy,
        Whose hand and heart combine,
In brave and excellent employ
        As radiantly as mine!
But oh the weary, dreary day,
        The wear and tear and irk
Of countless souls who cannot say:
        'I love my work.'

# CONTENTMENT

Bed and bread are all I need
       In my happy day;
Love of Nature is my creed,
       Unto her I pray;
Sun and sky my spirit feed
       On my happy way.

To no man I bow the head,
       None may master me;
I will eat my crust of bread
       Lauding liberty;
And upon my truckle bed
       Glory to be free.

You who grab for sordid gold,
       You who fight for fame,
Shiny dross your fingers hold,
       Empty is your aim.
—Soon we fatten graveyard mould,
       Rich and poor the same.

So from world of want and woe
       I retreat with dread;
Tuned to Nature glad I go
       With my bite of bread:
Praising God I lay me low
       On my truckle bed.

# THE PARTING

Sky's a-waxin' grey,
Got to be a-goin';
Gittin' on my way,
Where?  I ain't a-knowin'.
Fellers, no more jokes,
Fun an' frisky greetin'—
So long, all you folks,
Been nice our meetin'.

Sky's a-growin' dark,
Have to be a-startin'.
Feeble is the spark,
Pitiful the partin'.
Family an' all,
Thanks for joy I owe you;
Gotta take my call;
Been sweet to know you.

Sky's a-mighty black,
Close my heart's to breakin'.
Lonesome is the track
I must now be takin'.
Lordy, be You nigh,
Now's my time to prove you . . .
Life, good-bye, good-bye,—
Been grand to love you!

## L'ENVOI

Only a rhymer, so I am,
      Lone in the market place;
I shrink, and no one cares a damn
      Though tears corrode my face.
The hollows of my cheeks they track,
      Symbolic of vain hope;
My hands are grimed because I lack
      The price of soap.

Only a rhymer! How my breeks
      Let in the Winter wind;
One of my shoes obscenely leaks,
      My coat is safety pinned.
Although my neb drips bead on bead,
      No handkerchief have I;
My lips are blue, but none have heed
      My songs to buy.

Only a rhymer,—just a chiel
      Spewed from the land of Burns,
A wastrel and a ne'er-do-weel,
      From whom the public turns.
Alas! It is too late to mend
      The error of my ways,
So I will jingle to the end
      Of all my days.